PHARAOHS, PROPHETS & PLAGUES

GOING FROM CAPTIVITY TO THE PROMISED LIFE

DANIEL MATEOLA

FOREWORD BY TOMI ARAYOMI

PUBLICATIONS

PHARAOHS, PROPHETS & PLAGUES

Published by

Daniel Olugbenga Mateola
Kingdom Faith Ministries International

41 Blundells Road, Bradville, Milton Keynes
MK13 7HD, United Kingdom
Email: info@kfmi.org.uk
Websites: www.kfmi.org.uk

ISBN: 978-1-5136-7488-9

First printing: June 2021

Cover Design / book layout: Imaginovation Ltd.

Manufactured in the United Kingdom

ENDORSEMENTS

"Apostle Daniel, in his book Pharaohs, Prophets, and Plagues, cuts to the heart of the current social and political issues of our time. His message, from the heart of the Spirit of God is that we, the church, MUST turn away from fear and have faith in our God like never before lest we turn pharaohs into prophets whose false prophesies become self-fulfilling in our lives and in our nations. God is using the challenges and sufferings of our time to reveal to us where we are at. He desires that we receive his redirection and not only get back to faith, but also recover what was stolen, and receive a restored authority for advancing the kingdom in our day. We are the people of the living God!

Dr Kim Maas
Founder of Kim Maas Ministries, USA
Author of Prophetic Community: God's Call for All to Minister in His Gifts, and the forthcoming The Way of the Kingdom: Seizing the Time For a great Move of God (Chosen Books).

This is a timely book that presents to us the reality of what we are dealing with today and the keys to activate results by faith. It really showed that Apostle Daniel Mateola caught the revelation from the Holy Spirit concerning the pattern of how Pharaohs, Prophets and Plagues functioned in the word of

God and their role in our world today. The book also showed that regardless of how far we have been on the journey of faith, we can still receive hope and see our faith rejuvenated again. For without faith, we cannot please God. To both young and old in faith, you will definitely not be disappointed by reading this precious book. Thanks, Daniel Mateola, for blessing us with the NOW message from the heart of God.

Pastor Lola Oyebade
Senior Pastor, House On The Rock International Church London UK

"Pharaohs, Prophets and Plagues" is a must read! And I cannot think of anyone more qualified to write this than Apostle Daniel Mateola. What I have observed in knowing him for the last few years is that he carries the anointing of the 'sons of Issachar' who understood the times of seasons. I believe that the revelations he received and put into writing are going to remain relevant for many years to come if Jesus tarries. Indeed, God's children will need to navigate through future challenges that will hit the world with much stronger faith and better understanding of the major actors behind the scenes."

The prophetic revelation in this book will impart to you, wisdom to get rid of the spirits of fear, build your faith and to learn to better discern seasons and events in the world.

Truly we must prepare to handle future crisis better than we did with the 2020 pandemic, lockdowns, and its consequences.

Paul Dewar

Founder, Reachout Power Ministries, UK

TABLE OF CONTENTS

DEDICATION

To God be the glory, great things He has done. This book is dedicated to my lord, saviour, and redeemer 'King Jesus'. The one who left His royal status, abode, authority, power and glory to come into the world to die for me that I may be restored to my royal status, authority, power and glory in His kingdom.

ACKNOWLEDGEMENTS

To Ruth Adetilewa Mateola, I want to say thank you for sharing last twenty-seven years with me and blessing me with three wonderful children. You have continued to inspire me with your dedication and hard work concerning your ministry initiatives.

To my children, Jeremiah, Jeiel and Destiny, thank you for being good children and not overwhelming me with too much that I am able to serve God, His people and even to get the chance to write.

To my parents, Mr. Akinbowale Mateola & Mrs. Christianah Mateola, thank you for giving me a sound education and a strong foundation for life. You have deposited in me the knowledge and fear of God which has helped shape my life and character. Consider this book as one of the fruits of your labour.

Special thanks to the entire staff and congregants of the Kingdom Faith Ministries International movement worldwide. You have been an incredible kingdom family to me.

FOREWORD

I have had the esteemed privilege of being one of the first to get a copy of this book and I could not be more thrilled to be nominated to forward such a fantastic masterpiece.

Apostle Daniel Mateola is a very dear friend of mine and a co labourer in the United Kingdom. I have watched him personally outwork the kingdom life in his family and ministry. I have known his great joy to serve the body of Christ and his great sorrow to see Christ formed perfectly in the saints around the world. He not only demonstrates this in how he leads his church but how he has raised his amazing God-fearing children, which is perhaps arguably his and his wife's pastor Ruth's greatest achievement and one noteworthy of imitation.

Pharaohs, Prophets and Plagues is a word 'timely!' It represents a great intermission in the theatre of life for us to breath and retrospectively retract our preconceived notions about what is actually happening in our world. Its narrator is not Apostle Daniel, but it is God and Apostle Daniel becomes the scribe of our universal arbiter to write His narrative on what is going on.

Yes, we have all heard what the news is saying but this book calls into question whether or not we have really been hearing the news or the narrative. It draws from scripture and the unction of the prophet that lives within this amazing man of God to help the reader see covid, globalism and our elites through the lens of Jehovah. What I love most about this book is it not only narrates God's story but provides for us our crucial role to play in the public forum so that what was intended to be a participatory process doesn't become a monologue told by world systems with the church on its back foot reacting but proactively posturing herself for arguably her greatest hour!

He could not represent this book more and be more thrilled at what it is going to do in you to charge you and recommission the body of Christ to be effective. Early in 2021, I gave a prophetic word that the Lord says 'church, you have 9 years left!' Not 9 years till the return of Christ but 9 years to halt the spirit of falsehood that was going to rise up in the Nation. Shortly After that world leaders from all over the world chimed in unison 'we have 9 years left!' I believe that this book is a roadmap for the church for the next 9 years.

Tomi Arayomi
Apostle/Prophet, RIG NATION, UK & Global

INTRODUCTION

The year is 2020, the beginning of a new decade. Many authentic prophets of God had declared that we were entering a new era and not just a new decade, yet many of us had no idea what this year would bring. We had not expected that before the end of the first quarter, we would have started experiencing earth-shaking events.

These shakings came fast as we began to hear news about an outbreak of some sort of virus in China and in a matter of weeks, different countries started reporting the first cases of this unknown virus that could kill anyone prematurely.

From being an epidemic in a province in China, the situation was soon classified by the World Health Organization (WHO) as a global pandemic. Not long after that, countries started declaring national lockdowns, social and economic lives became affected, fear set in as many were concerned about the possibility of contacting this unknown virus or should we say plague.

God's covenant children started experiencing varied emotions since governments declared lockdown of churches too. Some preachers began to preach their version of eschatology (the study of the end times).

Interestingly, this did not stir up faith in the hearts of many saints, rather they began to fear, even more, the probability of untimely death. The rest of us had to step-up our prayer lives as we stormed heaven in search of answers. If you can understand, people like myself with a pastoral office had no choice, we had to bring word of comfort and direction to those God called us to care for.

I must confess that I was also searching the internet for what the men and women of God I respected were saying, particularly what the prophets had to say. I have always believed that prophets are called to hear the NOW word of God and to share it with the body of Christ. Unfortunately, this search was unfruitful, I soon discovered that many of those I expected to be voices were silent, and so I concluded that they were also trying to figure out what was going on in the world. Everyone was being careful not to announce false prophecies.

I got so frustrated one day that I did a short video nugget on Facebook and YouTube. It was more like a rant where I lamented about the deafening silence of church leaders. Following this rant, I got a call from one of my pastor friends and it was during our conversation that I heard the Lord say to me quietly in my inner man, "Son, why are looking to other men to hear what is on my heart?"

That hit me hard. It also dawned on me that I had entertained a mindset of believing that I was still some sort of junior man of God and needed to search for those I considered to be senior for what God is saying.

That encounter with the word of God quickly slapped some spiritual sense into me. I knew I had to be willing to pay the price to seek Him to hear from Him for myself and for those whom He has put in my pastoral care. It was my pursuit that led me to begin to hear from the Lord what became the main subject of this book.

One day, in the last week of March 2020, during my devotion, the Lord took me to the book of Exodus and began to teach me by His Spirit the story of Moses, Pharaoh, and the Plagues. He then began to give me revelations of what was going on in our world using the analogy of Pharaohs, Prophets and Plagues. These revelations began to unfold more and more as I started teaching it to the congregation I pastor (Kingdom Faith Ministries International, UK).

I believe with all my heart that the concepts and truths that the Holy Spirit taught me and is still teaching carried me, my biological and church family through that exceedingly difficult season in our lives. Our testimony as a church family is that by the end of the year 2020, we had experienced no losses or death. For many months, the church continued to take advantage of loopholes in government guidelines, still, God kept the plague away from our entire church family.

Rather than experience job losses because of the economic challenges, members of our church family got better jobs, raises and bonuses, and other kinds of financial breakthroughs. We had more members buy their own homes than any other year since we have been in existence. To top it, even the church bank balance was significantly higher than what it was the previous year.

I have written this book under the leading of the Spirit

of the Lord as He taught me that I was accountable for the revelations I received and needed to share them for others to benefit. The Lord also made it clear to me that these revelations were going to remain relevant for many years to come if Jesus tarries. God's children will need it as we navigate through future challenges that will hit our world.

Remember the question regarding experiencing challenges in life is not a matter of "if" but rather of "when". Challenges will come whether you like it or not. I have lived long enough to know that you do not have to invite them.

However, the key thing is getting ready for them in advance. You can be that wise person Jesus spoke about in Matthew chapter seven that prepared for the storm by building on a rock. I pray that this book blesses and empowers you for a breakthrough in your future regardless of the challenges and difficulties ahead.

CHAPTER 1

THE PHARAOHS

"¹⁷ For the Scripture says to the Pharaoh, "For this very purpose I have raised you up, that I may show My power in you, and that My name may be declared in all the earth."
Romans 9:17 (NKJV)

The Origin of Pharaohs

Ancient Egypt was one of the greatest and most powerful civilizations in the world. It lasted for over 3000 years from 3150 BC to 30 BC. This powerful entity was located along the Nile River in Northeast Africa which was the source of much of its wealth. The Nile is also the longest river in the world flowing northward for nearly 4,200 miles.

To talk about Pharaohs, their origins, and their great

powers as Egyptian rulers, we have to dig up interesting historical information about Egypt itself.

In the early period of civilization, during the Old Kingdom, Egypt was referred to as Kemet (pronounced Kermit). It can also be spelt as Kmt, which means the 'Black Land'. They called themselves "remetch en Kermet", which means the "People of the Black Land," a term that refers to the rich soil found in the Nile Valley and Delta. The historical records of ancient Egypt begin with it as a unified state which occurred sometime around 3150 BC.

The Egyptian culture, customs, artistic expression, architecture, and social structure were closely tied to religion, remarkably stable, and changed little for nearly 3000 years.

Egypt looked the same geographically in 3000 B.C. as it does in the 21st century. The country was mostly covered by desert but along the Nile River was a fertile swath that proved — and still proves—a life source for many Egyptians. For almost 30 centuries—from its unification around 3100 B.C. to its conquest by Alexander the Great in 332 B.C.—Ancient Egypt was the preeminent civilization in the Mediterranean world.

From the great pyramids of the Old Kingdom through the military conquests of the New Kingdom, Egypt's majesty has long entranced archaeologists and historians, and created a vibrant field of study called Egyptology.

The main sources of information about Ancient Egypt are the many monuments, objects and artefacts that have been recovered from archaeological sites, covered with hieroglyphs that have only recently been deciphered. The picture that emerges is of a culture with few equals in the beauty of its art, the accomplishment of its architecture and the richness of its religious traditions.

Now that we have some historical information about the greatness of Ancient Egypt, let us take a closer look at the Pharaohs, their origin and power.

First, I want to clearly state that Pharaohs were kings and were not elected leaders like Presidents and Prime Ministers today. This means that they had absolute power to rule their kingdom as they saw fit. Nobody voted them in and nobody could vote them out. As kings, their words became decrees, and they did not need any form of congress to agree to their words before they became law. Not only did Pharaohs have absolute power, but they also controlled all the wealth of their kingdom which included human and material resources.

> ...Pharaohs were kings and were not elected leaders like Presidents and Prime Ministers today.

The pharaonic period in which Egypt was ruled by a pharaoh, is dated from the 32nd century BC when Upper and Lower Egypt were unified until the country fell under Macedonian rule in 332 BC.

According to Manetho an Egyptian priest who lived in the Ptolemaic Kingdom in the early third century BC, the first pharaoh was Menes, but archaeological findings support the view that the first ruler to claim to have united the two lands was Narmer, the final king of the Naqada III period. His name is known primarily from the famous Narmer Palette, whose scenes have been interpreted as the act of uniting Upper and Lower Egypt. Menes is now thought to be one of the titles of Hor-Aha, the second pharaoh of the First Dynasty.

Pharaohs in The Bible

The first thing I discovered when I started researching pharaohs in the bible was how often the word Pharaoh appeared in the bible, particularly in the Old Testament. The word appeared two hundred and forty-three times and I believe this was significant considering that there were many different nations and kings covered in bible stories and only the kings of Egypt were called Pharaohs. The first mention of a Pharaoh was in the days of Abraham when he first journeyed down to Egypt during a time that the world was experiencing a famine recorded in Genesis twelve.

> *14 So it was, when Abram came into Egypt, that the Egyptians saw the woman, that she was very beautiful. 15 The princes of Pharaoh also saw her and commended her to Pharaoh. And the woman was taken to Pharaoh's house. 16 He treated Abram well for her sake. He had*

sheep, oxen, male donkeys, male and female servants,
female donkeys, and camels.

Genesis 12:14-16

If you are not familiar with this scripture, here is a summary of what happened. The Pharaoh took interest in Sarai and decided to keep her as a wife in his palace. This resulted in him having an encounter with God in a dream after suffering a plague, which caused him to find out that Sarai was another man's (a prophet) wife. Consequently, he handed Sarai back to her husband along with some gifts as compensation.

The second time another Pharaoh was mentioned in the bible was in the days of Joseph the grandson of Abraham. You will find the story about this Pharaoh and the events that preceded the rise of Israel as a nation called by God to be His chosen people recorded in Genesis chapter thirty-seven to the end.

The third record about another Pharaoh is in Exodus, the second book of Moses. We are introduced to this Pharaoh as one who did not remember Joseph or the great his God did for Egypt during the reign of this Pharaoh's predecessor.

[8] Now there arose a new king over Egypt, who did not
know Joseph. [9] And he said to his people, "Look, the
people of the children of Israel are more and mightier
than we; [10] come, let us deal shrewdly with them, lest

they multiply, and it happen, in the event of war, that
they also join our enemies and fight against us, and so
go up out of the land."

Exodus 1:8-10

I cannot write about all that the Pharaohs of the bible did in this book, but I can extrapolate some truths that are noteworthy about Pharaohs in the bible.

1. Pharaohs are kings and have absolute power. This means they control the human and material resources in their kingdom and do as they please.

> Pharaohs, though worshippers of false gods were not outside of God's reach.

2. Pharaohs, though worshippers of false gods were not outside of God's reach. God will get their attention even if it means using dreams.

3. Pharaohs can enjoy God's divine favour to the extent that their kingdom becomes great. Note that the kingdom of Egypt was favoured by God under the first Pharaohs such that they thrived during the first three famines that devastated the rest of the world in those days.

4. Pharaohs can also be accessible to the devil just as they can be to God. The big issue is that whomever they choose to listen to would have significant impact in the life of many because of the influence they already have.

5. Pharaohs can be seduced by the devil to thirst for more

wealth and power regardless of what they already have. I will share a bit more about this power seduction issue later in this chapter.

As mentioned earlier Egypt was a significant kingdom and world power for many centuries hence, we can assume that there were many more immensely powerful Pharaohs that existed and left their mark in history.

The Good, Bad and Ugly Pharaohs

Let us take another look at the first three pharaohs mentioned in the bible. This time we will examine their actions as good, bad or ugly. The first was the Pharaoh in the time of Abram (later renamed Abraham by God). This was the Pharaoh that unintentionally took Abram's wife into his palace. He did it because Abram had lied that Sarai (later renamed Sarah by God) was his sister when she was his wife. The story goes on to tell us that God intervened in the matter on Abram's behalf to help him get his wife back—another action revealing the mercy of God even though Abram was in the wrong.

> ¹⁵ *The princes of Pharaoh also saw her and commended her to Pharaoh. And the woman was taken to Pharaoh's house.* ¹⁶ *He treated Abram well for her sake. He had sheep, oxen, male donkeys, male and female servants, female donkeys, and camels.* ¹⁷ *But the LORD plagued Pharaoh and his house with great plagues because of*

7

Sarai, Abram's wife. [18] *And Pharaoh called Abram and said, "What is this you have done to me? Why did you not tell me that she was your wife?* [19] *Why did you say, 'She is my sister'? I might have taken her as my wife. Now therefore, here is your wife; take her and go your way."* [20] *So Pharaoh commanded his men concerning him; and they sent him away, with his wife and all that he had.*

Genesis 12:15-20

We can say that this Pharaoh qualifies as good by biblical definition. He must have somehow sought God concerning the plague and was informed of what he had done regarding Sarai. He had every right to be angry with Abram for lying that Sarai was his sister and for receiving gifts from him when he knew he had deceived him. Instead, this Pharaoh enquired of Abram to confirm that she was indeed his wife and then returned her to him. He also ensured that Abram left Egypt with all his prosperity.

The second Pharaoh existed in the time that Joseph was taken into Egypt as a slave. This Pharaoh had a dream about seven fat cows and seven lean cows where the fat ones were eaten by the lean ones, he also had a similar dream regarding seven full heads of grain and seven withered heads. In his quest to seek for a man to interpret his dreams, he met Joseph the grandson of Abraham.

Joseph was anointed by God with the gift of dreams and their interpretation and was able to interpret his dreams.

Not only was he able to do that, through the gift of 'Word of Wisdom', but he also offered Pharaoh the solution to the impending crisis God wanted them to avert for the benefit of Egypt.

I am amazed by the grace of God and how He can choose to show His unmerited favour to those who do not know or worship Him such as Egypt, a country that worshipped idols at that time.

From this, I believe God had more than Egypt on His mind when He gave these dreams to Pharaoh. He wanted to preserve the lives of many people from other lands that will be affected by the famine. God divinely intervened in the affairs of Egypt with the future kingdom of Israel in mind to ensure the fulfilment of the covenant He made with Abraham. The story goes on to tell us that this Pharaoh received Joseph's counsel and rewarded him with the highest position in Egypt. Joseph was promoted to become second in command to the Pharaoh himself. Joseph's promotion reveals a powerful principle from the scriptures. Any covenant child of God that obeys God and serves faithfully with his or her gift will end up being promoted by God and ultimately by man.

> Any covenant child of God that obeys God and serves faithfully with his or her gift will end up being promoted by God and ultimately by man.

37 So the advice was good in the eyes of Pharaoh and in the eyes of all his servants. 38 And Pharaoh said to his servants, "Can we find such a one as this, a man in whom is the Spirit of God?"

39 Then Pharaoh said to Joseph, "Inasmuch as God has shown you all this, there is no one as discerning and wise as you. 40 You shall be over my house, and all my people shall be ruled according to your word; only in regard to the throne will I be greater than you." 41 And Pharaoh said to Joseph, "See, I have set you over all the land of Egypt."

Genesis 41:37-41

Joseph did not only become second in command to Pharaoh, he was also put in charge of Egypt's economy. Much later Joseph's father and siblings came to join him in Egypt and Pharaoh received them warmly and blessed them with the land of Goshen to settle in. Life was good for them.

When you consider this aspect of the story about this Pharaoh, you will be tempted to call him good. But you need to look at some other things that he did. When the famine hit, this Pharaoh and Joseph were ready to tackle it since they had been storing grains for seven years and had built massive storage facilities. Here are a few things this Pharaoh did that put him in the 'bad' grade.

1. He did not warn any other king or nation about the coming famine so that they may store some grains too because

10

he wanted all nations and people to be at his mercy when the famine hit.

2. He systematically allowed money to fail or become worthless because of extreme inflation resulting from demand outweighing supply. He had control over the stored grains and could drive their prices up until the money in many people's hands lost value.

3. He tactfully took over possession of the wealth of the people of Egypt and not only did they lose their flocks, herds and other animals, they also lost their farms. In other words, they lost their ability to earn a living independent of the state of Egypt. This can be likened to destroying small businesses and taking the people's ability to make a living independent of their government in the 21st century.

4. He also enslaved the Egyptians. It got so bad that they were working the farmlands that were formerly theirs as servants of this Pharaoh and were commanded to give up twenty per cent of their harvest for him.

[13] Now there was no bread in all the land; for the famine was very severe, so that the land of Egypt and the land of Canaan languished because of the famine. [14] And Joseph gathered up all the money that was found in the land of Egypt and in the land of Canaan, for the grain which they bought; and Joseph brought the money into Pharaoh's house.

[15] So when the money failed in the land of Egypt and in

11

the land of Canaan, all the Egyptians came to Joseph and said, "Give us bread, for why should we die in your presence? For the money has failed." ¹⁶ Then Joseph said, "Give your livestock, and I will give you bread for your livestock, if the money is gone."

¹⁷ So they brought their livestock to Joseph, and Joseph gave them bread in exchange for the horses, the flocks, the cattle of the herds, and for the donkeys. Thus he [b] fed them with bread in exchange for all their livestock that year.

¹⁸ When that year had ended, they came to him the next year and said to him, "We will not hide from my lord that our money is gone; my lord also has our herds of livestock. There is nothing left in the sight of my lord but our bodies and our lands.

¹⁹ Why should we die before your eyes, both we and our land? Buy us and our land for bread, and we and our land will be servants of Pharaoh; give us seed, that we may live and not die, that the land may not be desolate." ²⁰ Then Joseph bought all the land of Egypt for Pharaoh; for every man of the Egyptians sold his field, because the famine was severe upon them. So the land became Pharaoh's.

Genesis 47:13-20

I am sure you will agree with me that this Pharaoh was a bad man. He enslaved his people forgetting that if not for God that graced him with the dream, he would have perished in the famine also. He who has received grace and mercy must learn to gracious and merciful to others.

Let us examine the third Pharaoh in power when Moses was born. This is the one I will call "ugly" and show you why.

> [8] *Now there arose a new king over Egypt, who did not know Joseph.* [9] *And he said to his people, "Look, the people of the children of Israel are more and mightier than we;* [10] *come, let us deal shrewdly with them, lest they multiply, and it happen, in the event of war, that they also join our enemies and fight against us, and so go up out of the land."*
>
> [11] *Therefore they set taskmasters over them to afflict them with their burdens. And they built for Pharaoh supply cities, Pithom and Raamses.* [12] *But the more they afflicted them, the more they multiplied and grew. And they were in dread of the children of Israel.*
>
> [13] *So the Egyptians made the children of Israel serve with rigor.* [14] *And they made their lives bitter with hard bondage—in mortar, in brick, and in all manner of service in the field. All their service in which they made them serve was with rigor.*
>
> Exodus 1:8-14

He who has received grace and mercy must learn to gracious and merciful to others.

Our first introduction to this Pharaoh confirms that he was a bad man. The eighth verse of Exodus chapter one states that this Pharaoh did not remember Joseph. It is not that there was no historical information passed down to him, instead, he chose to disregard Joseph's contribution (a Hebrew) to the survival of Egypt in the time of famine and the prosperity enjoyed by the kingdom afterwards. He intentionally decided to forget all of that so he could carry out his ugly plans to impoverish and enslave Joseph's descendants. Let us take a closer look at what this Pharaoh did.

- He chose to disregard the good deeds of others before him which made him an ungrateful man.
- He chose to deal shrewdly with Joseph's descendants, setting taskmasters over them and afflicting them with burdens.
- He chose to completely enslave the Hebrews causing their lives to be bitter with hard bondage.
- He ordered the killing of male Hebrew children at birth by the midwives who were supposed to ensure their safe delivery.
- He also ordered the killing of all male children who escaped his initial plans through the midwives to be killed. This is an ugly and wicked move to ensure that the Hebrews at some point will no longer have male children that could father more children.

From the five points mentioned above, you see that this Pharaoh was worse than the Pharaoh in Joseph's time. He was fully possessed by a demonic spirit that was determined to annihilate the Hebrews before the prophetic word of God to Abraham could come to pass. Remember that in Genesis chapter fifteen, God gave the Hebrew patriarch the prophetic word that He was going to make his descendants a great nation and give them the promised land.

> *⁴ And behold, the word of the LORD came to him, saying, "This one shall not be your heir, but one who will come from your own body shall be your heir." ⁵ Then He brought him outside and said, "Look now toward heaven, and count the stars if you are able to number them." And He said to him, "So shall your descendants be."*
>
> Genesis 15:4-5

> *¹⁸ On the same day the LORD made a covenant with Abram, saying: "To your descendants I have given this land, from the river of Egypt to the great river, the River Euphrates— 19 the Kenites, the Kenezzites, the Kadmonites, 20 the Hittites, the Perizzites, the Rephaim, 21 the Amorites, the Canaanites, the Girgashites, and the Jebusites."*
>
> Genesis 15:18-21

At this point, I want to encourage you to be fervent in prayer when you receive a good prophetic word. Never forget

15

that the devil is not omniscient and hence does not know many things until it is spoken or revealed to him.

Note that prophetic words are usually followed by demonic opposition, it is no wonder that Abraham waited for over two decades to receive the son God promised him, and his son Isaac also waited for two decades before he had his twin sons Esau and Jacob who was prophesied to one day become the father of the nation Israel.

The 21st Century Pharaohs

You must be wondering what I mean by this subheading since Egypt is no longer a kingdom, but a country and their leaders are no longer called Pharaohs. Cleopatra (69 BCE–30 BCE) as Cleopatra VII Philopater was the last of the Ptolemy dynasty of Egyptian rulers, and the last Pharaoh of Egypt, ending a dynastic rule of some 5,000 years.

> ...Prophetic words are usually followed by demonic opposition...

The people I want to introduce to you as 21st century Pharaohs are not even Egyptians neither are they presidents or prime ministers of nations. The people that the spirit of the Lord likened to Pharaohs as He gave me the revelation of this book are men and women with incredible wealth, power, and influence in today's world.

They are people that have held monopolies in their areas

of enterprise owning large corporations that extend to almost every first-world nation and for some, second and third world nations. They employ hundreds of thousands of people and control other influential people including presidents and prime ministers.

One of the reasons they have politicians and leaders in their pocket is because they are extremely wealthy. These people I call 21st century Pharaohs are all multi-billionaires with more money in their possession than any man or woman needs to spend in their lifetime. Regarding events in our world, I believe that there are at least three groups of people.

- Those who are not aware of what is happening. These are ignorant people, do not care or are burdened with issues of life that they cannot see anything else.
- Those who know what is happening in the world but feel helpless and hopeless about making a difference. They watch things happen but do nothing.
- Those who make things happen. These are the movers and shakers of the world. Scrutiny will reveal their involvement with every major happening.

In the third group of people that make things happen, I believe there are many subgroups or sublevels. The highest by far is where you will find the 21st century Pharaohs. Not many people are in that group, but their impact is significant. In the year 2020, when we first experienced the outbreak of the virus in different countries, the pharaohs were quick to step in to control and manipulate happenings to ensure that the outcomes work in their favour. During a crisis, 21st century Pharaohs look for ways to take advantage of the crisis to increase their wealth, power, and influence.

I can also use the analogy of "the good, the bad and the ugly" to describe 21st century Pharaohs. The good ones use their wealth and power to do good and are willing to respond correctly to God's warning. These types of Pharaohs are men who still understand that it is by the grace of God that they acquired their immense wealth, power, and influence. I decided not to mention names, hopeful that you can figure out a few examples. The bad 21st century pharaohs are those who do what the Pharaoh in the time of Joseph did. At the beginning of the current pandemic, they quickly positioned themselves to do the following:

- With foresight, they had quickly developed ways of doing business online long before the pandemic and lockdowns. They then encouraged governments to enforce the lockdown resulting in increased revenue for them while they watch others suffer.
- They sort means to destroy competitors that required walk-in customers or physical stores to make money. They pulled all necessary strings to sustain and prolong the lockdown.
- Some identified as "Globalists" took advantage of the plague to begin to forcefully implement their plan for a

total economic reset without any care for those who will be impacted negatively, (e.g., people who will lose their businesses, jobs and hence livelihood).

- Some Pharaohs had taken over lands owned by poor farmers just like the Pharaoh in Joseph's time. In September 2020 during the global pandemic, the Indian government passed a new law to allow the selling of farms without government oversight. These poor farmers have been demonstrating since then as they have become aware of who is buying their lands. A credible news source claimed that over five thousand farmers have since committed suicide because of unmanageable debt.

- Other pharaohs with immensely large and powerful media outlets began several campaigns with the intent to lie and program people's mind to see things from their point of view to achieve their selfish and sometimes sinister motives. Some of these Pharaohs have made themselves the arbiters of truth putting their own fact-checkers on all their media platforms and cancelling anyone that tries to share anything different from what they want people to believe.

Now to the worst group that I refer to as the ugly. These are the pharaohs with mainly demonically motivated ideas and concepts. During the pandemic they began to implement ideas like the ugly pharaoh in Moses' time. Here are few things that the ugly Pharaohs were up to.

- They used the lockdown and other rules such as social distancing to achieve their goal of social re-engineering with a desire to reduce human interaction.
- They introduced ways to modify the genetic composition of men under the disguise of medical solutions to a pandemic. This genetic modification is to happen through some of the vaccines introduced e.g., the vaccine that uses mRNA technology. The messenger RNA communicates with human cells and instruct them to produce certain proteins abnormally to recreate the coronavirus and then antibodies to fight it.
- They introduced sick ideas of population control by deliberating executing plans to see to the death of people of certain races and geographical locations. Again, these ugly Pharaohs disguise themselves as those who want to save lives but, they believe in eugenics.

Eugenics is the study of or belief in the possibility of improving the qualities of the human species or a human population, especially by such means as discouraging reproduction by persons having genetic defects or presumed to have inheritable undesirable traits (negative eugenics) or encouraging reproduction by persons presumed to have inheritable desirable traits (positive eugenics).

The Power Seduction

From the beginning of time, we were introduced to the

greatest source of evil influence on the earth. We were also exposed to one of the devil's major weapons for executing evil schemes and getting men to participate in it. Let us looks at a few verses in Genesis chapter three.

> Now the serpent was more cunning than any beast of the field which the Lord God had made. And he said to the woman, "Has God indeed said, 'You shall not eat of every tree of the garden'?" ² And the woman said to the serpent, "We may eat the fruit of the trees of the garden; ³ but of the fruit of the tree which is in the midst of the garden, God has said, 'You shall not eat it, nor shall you touch it, lest you die.' ⁴ Then the serpent said to the woman, "You will not surely die. ⁵ For God knows that in the day you eat of it your eyes will be opened, and you will be like God, knowing good and evil."
>
> Genesis 3:1-4

From the verses above we see that the serpent's tool for deceiving man into rebellion against God was to seduce him with lust for power and control. I call it "The Power Seduction". It was this craze for great wealth, power, and influence that produced the bad and ugly Pharaohs in the bible. Unfortunately, this power is still the devil's tool for the creation of the 21st century Pharaohs.

If you study their lives, you will notice that they were

fortunate men and women who became highly successful in business and enterprise by God's grace. Most of them got ideas and concept meant to help meet major human needs. The solutions they developed helped them become incredibly wealthy as people are always willing to pay for goods or services that meet their needs or solve their problems.

...The serpent's tool for deceiving man into rebellion against God was to seduce him with lust for power and control.

Unfortunately, they get seduced by the enemy to desire more wealth and begin to destroy their competitors in the process. Then they get to the stage where the wealth and influence from their monopoly or market domination are not enough. The seduction draws them to seek political or governmental power and influence and they continue to fall for it until they begin to desire power and influence on a global scale. It is at this point that they begin to see themselves as little gods and thus begin to attract God's judgment which is always preceded by warnings through His prophets.

In a later chapter I will talk about the clash between Pharaohs and Prophets, but first let us look at understanding prophets, who they are and why they are a critical part of God's response to dealing with bad and ugly Pharaohs.

Prayer:

Lord, I thank You for the divine insight and revelation that I have received about Pharaohs and particularly the seduction to become a bad or ugly one. First, I ask that you deliver me from every type of oppression or suppression I am may be experiencing because of bad and ugly Pharaohs in my world.

Lord, grant me discernment to identify their evil works and to protect myself from them. I also pray for the grace to help others be free from the evil claws of these men. Father teach me humility and contentment that I will not be a victim of satanic seductions to become a Pharaoh. Finally, I pray that you will search my heart, take away every wrong ambition and anything that could make me fall for demonic seduction. Lord lead me not into temptation and please deliver me from evil in Jesus' name. Amen!

CHAPTER 2

THE PROPHETS

⁶ And God said to him in a dream, "Yes, I know that you did this in the integrity of your heart. For I also withheld you from sinning against Me; therefore I did not let you touch her. ⁷ Now therefore, restore the man's wife; for he is a prophet, and he will pray for you and you shall live. But if you do not restore her, know that you shall surely die, you and all who are yours."

Genesis 20:6-7

THE SCRIPTURAL REFERENCE I have chosen to start this chapter with is the one where the word "Prophet" appears for the first time in the bible. I also chose it because the character referred to as a prophet here is one that many Christians today will not immediately list as one of the bible prophets.

The truth is many in the body of Christ today do not understand the office or mantle of the prophet. Some believe that prophets only existed in the Old Testament and are no longer relevant or required under the new covenant.

I will discuss this further when we get to a sub-chapter where I write about the 21st-century prophet. For now, let me attempt to define who a prophet is.

Who Is A Prophet?

...A prophet as, "one who utters divinely inspired revelations; gifted with more than ordinary spiritual and moral insight...

The simplest definition of the word 'prophet' I have found is from the Merriam Webster Dictionary. It defines a prophet as, "one who utters divinely inspired revelations; gifted with more than ordinary spiritual and moral insight and who foretells future events".

Of course, there are many more definitions of the word in other dictionaries but for now, let us stick with the one I have shared with you.

Looking at this definition from a non-religious book, we can extract the following truths about a prophet for everyone's clarity (Christian or non-Christian).

- Prophets hear from God.
- Prophets can foretell future events.

- Prophets are empowered to hear or see beyond the natural abilities of men.
- Prophets are a type of God's mouthpiece to reveal his wishes and plans to men.

Next, let me give you the biblical perspective of the word 'Prophet'. First, let us look at the original Hebrew word that was translated into the word Prophet in its first use in the Old Testament. The Hebrew word is 'Nabi' also spelt as 'Nabiy' but pronounced 'Naw-bee'.

This word simply means spokesman or speaker. Taking earlier dictionary definitions into consideration, I can expand this word 'Nabi' to mean one empowered to be a spokesman for God.

As I mentioned earlier, some Christians today will admit that they never saw Abraham as God's prophet, but God says he was one. This tells me that Abraham must have been declaring what God revealed to him about the plans to birth a nation through him. I can imagine Abraham prophesying over his wife Sarah that she will have a child even when she had passed the childbearing age.

Before I get you excited about the grace prophets embody to declare powerful words that cause miraculous manifestations, let me expose more truths to you about the different types of prophets and how they operate.

Types of Prophets

I am almost certain that if many Christians today were asked about the different types of prophets, their response will be something like, "major prophets and minor prophets". Others may answer, "Old Testament prophets and New Testament prophets". I know you may be reading this book and wondering what is wrong with that? Those are not the types of prophets in the bible. At best we can refer to them as classifications.

To discover the type of prophets in the bible, we must go back to the original languages that the books of the bible were written in to find the root words that were translated to the English version. It will help to reveal what type of prophet is referred to.

In the Old Testament, there are three Hebrew words translated into the English word "prophet". They are nabi, raáh (or roéh), and hozeh. Like we said before, Nabi means spokesman which is the most common word for a prophet. Apart from Abraham, there are many other examples of nabi prophets in the Old Testament.

> "The Lord sent **prophets** amongst them to lead them
> back to Him. They warned the people..."
>
> 2 Chronicles 24:19

Jeremiah is another example of a 'nabi' prophet. He was

28

asked by God to become a spokesman for Him to the people.

> ⁴ *Then the word of the Lord came to me, saying:*
> ⁵ *"Before I formed you in the womb, I knew you; Before you were born, I sanctified you; I ordained you a prophet to the nations."*
>
> Jeremiah 1:4-5

> *"The Lord said to Jeremiah: 'Stand in the gate of the Lord's temple and proclaim this message…'"*
>
> Jeremiah 7:1

In Samuel's time, another word raáh, meaning "seer", was introduced and occurred seven times about Samuel. A seer receives prophetic revelation in dreams and visions and can also distinguish God's messages embedded within creation.

> *Formerly in Israel, when a man went to inquire of God, he spoke thus: 'Come, let us go to the seer'; for he who is now called a prophet was formerly called a seer".*
>
> I Samuel 9:9

If you are unfamiliar with the scripture reference above, it was at the time when Kish (Saul's father) sent him and a servant in search of lost donkeys. They had been searching for some time without success at finding the stray animals.

Finally, after Saul suggested that they head back to avoid creating anxiety at home, his servant offered that they look for a seer (prophet) who would direct them to where the lost donkeys were. In other words, the servant had enough faith in the office of the prophet to believe that God gives them a supernatural vision to see things that are not visible in the natural. Indeed, Samuel proved him right by supernaturally seeing that the donkeys had returned home.

> [19] *Samuel answered Saul and said, "I am the seer. Go up before me to the high place, for you shall eat with me today; and tomorrow I will let you go and will tell you all that is in your heart. [20] But as for your donkeys that were lost three days ago, do not be anxious about them, for they have been found. And [e]on whom is all the desire of Israel? Is it not on you and on all your father's house?"*
>
> 1 Samuel 9:19-20

The third Hebrew word that I mentioned earlier 'hozeh', also means "seer" which is a synonym of raáh but a rarer Hebrew term that means, "to see in a vision". This word was used to describe the prophetic office of some of the Old Testament prophets like Gad who served in King David's time.

> [11] *Now when David arose in the morning, the word of the LORD came to the prophet Gad, David's seer, saying,*
>
> 2 Samuel 24:11

There is a place in the Old Testament where three prophets were mentioned, and the root Hebrew words used was different because the author was inspired by God to clearly distinguish the type of prophet they were.

> [29] *Now the acts of King David, first and last, indeed they are written in the book of Samuel the seer, in the book of Nathan the prophet, and in the book of Gad the seer,*
>
> 1 Chronicles 29:29

In the verse above, all these three words are used: "Samuel the seer (raáh), Nathan the prophet (nabi), Gad the seer (hozeh)". These three functions were carried over into the New Testament as well. The diversity of New Testament prophets is mostly centred on the prophet's measure or sphere of influence as well as how they primarily receive God's word.

Apart from how prophets receive God's word and how they declare it, there is also the idea of the level of influence that God desires for them to operate in. Some prophets operate mainly within the local church; others are graced to operate on a city-wide level while others operate on a national level. Beyond these, there are a few who are empowered to operate on a global level. They are led or instructed to prophesy about different nations, leaders and events by God.

31

Prophets in The Bible

As you can see, God has been raising, anointing, and using men as prophets from the beginning of time. From the Old Testament to the New Testament, there are so many examples of men and women that were used in the office of a prophet. Let me mention a few of them that made significant impact in their prophetic offices.

> ...God has been raising, anointing, and using men as prophets from the beginning of time.

We will talk about both the male and female prophets beginning with the latter. The label "prophetess" or "woman prophet" (něbî'āh) is attributed to five women in the Old Testament: Miriam (Exodus. 15:20), Deborah (Judges. 4:4), Huldah (2 Kings 22:14; 2 Chronicles. 34:22), Noadiah (Nehemiah. 6:14), and Isaiah's wife "the prophetess" (Isaiah. 8:3).

> ²⁰ Then Miriam the prophetess, the sister of Aaron, took the timbrel in her hand; and all the women went out after her with timbrels and with dances.
>
> Exodus 15:20

Miriam was Moses' elder sister used by God to preserve his life as the preordained prophet and deliverer of the Hebrews from bondage. I have known of the vital part she played in Moses' story since I was in Sunday school, but it was only recently that I found that she was also a prophet. The

32

Hebrew word 'Nbiyah' translated to prophetess in the text above is a derivative of the word 'nabi'. In other words, Miriam in this context was not just singing a song but was declaring the prophetic word of God as she was inspired through the song.

> ⁴ Now Deborah, a prophetess, the wife of Lapidoth, was judging Israel at that time. ⁵ And she would sit under the palm tree of Deborah between Ramah and Bethel in the mountains of Ephraim. And the children of Israel came up to her for judgment. ⁶ Then she sent and called for Barak the son of Abinoam from Kedesh in Naphtali, and said to him, "Has not the LORD God of Israel commanded, 'Go and]deploy troops at Mount Tabor; take with you ten thousand men of the sons of Naphtali and of the sons of Zebulun; ⁷ and against you I will deploy Sisera, the commander of Jabin's army, with his chariots and his multitude at the River Kishon; and I will deliver him into your hand'?"
>
> Judges 4:4-7

Deborah was also called by God to be a prophet. The word 'prophetess' in the above text is also the same word 'Nbiyah' in Hebrew which lets us know that she was a speaking prophet. Indeed, the text reveals Deborah in action as she declares the prophetic word of the Lord over Barak. Through this word, Barak was released to become the mighty leader to deliver Israel from the hands of their enemies once again.

> *36 Now there was one, Anna, a prophetess, the daughter of Phanuel, of the tribe of Asher. She was of a great age and had lived with a husband seven years from her virginity; 37 and this woman was a widow of about eighty-four years, who did not depart from the temple, but served God with fastings and prayers night and day. 38 And coming in that instant she gave thanks to the Lord and spoke of Him to all those who looked for redemption in Jerusalem.*
>
> Luke 2:36-38

Luke presents Anna as a "woman prophet" (prophetess), which is the same Greek word the Septuagint (the Greek translation of the Old Testament), uses to translate the Hebrew 'nbiyah' (Luke 2:36). Like the prophet Simeon who was paired with her, Anna is led by the Holy Spirit to speak about Jesus "to all who were looking for the redemption of Jerusalem," (2:38).

We will discover next some male prophets, two from the Old Testament and one from the New Testament.

> *29 Now the acts of King David, first and last, indeed they are written in the book of Samuel the seer, in the book of Nathan the prophet, and in the book of Gad the seer,*
>
> 1 Chronicles 29:29

You will recall that I said Samuel was a seer prophet (raáh) and Nathan was a speaking prophet (nabi). Interestingly, they both ministered during King David's reign.

Samuel was the seer that helped identify Saul as the first king of Israel and also pointed out David as the next king. The story of how David was chosen reveals the supernatural ability of a prophet to see what others cannot see. David's father was blind that when he was asked to bring out his sons for the selection of Israel's next king, he did not bother to call David.

He did not see the king in him, but Samuel did and not only did he operate as a personal prophet in David and Saul's lives, he was also a national prophet. He was endowed with the ability to see events concerning Israel before they happened. Every nation should pray for God's ordained prophets like Samuel to guide them in difficult times.

Nathan also operated in the office of a prophet like Samuel, but he was more of a spokesman for God in the life of David. There were several occasions when David would have missed God and it would have affected the destiny of Israel, but for Nathan.

Now it came to pass when the king was dwelling in his house, and the LORD had given him rest from all his enemies all around, ² that the king said to Nathan the prophet, "See now, I dwell in a house of cedar, but the ark of God dwells inside tent curtains." ³ Then Nathan said to the king, "Go, do all that is in your heart, for the

35

LORD is with you." ⁴ But it happened that night that the word of the LORD came to Nathan, saying, ⁵ "Go and tell My servant David, 'Thus says the LORD: "Would you build a house for Me to dwell in?...

¹² "When your days are fulfilled and you rest with your fathers, I will set up your seed after you, who will come from your body, and I will establish his kingdom. ¹³ He shall build a house for My name, and I will establish the throne of his kingdom forever.

2 Samuel 7:1-5, 12-13

Though God chose to use Samuel and Nathan in slightly different ways, both helped David and Israel to stay in God's will. Their prophetic ministries also clearly revealed God's heart concerning the selection of national leaders. I have heard many argue that God does not get involved with earthly governments and politics which is so far from true.

This argument became more popular in 2020 as some prophets chose to weigh in on the matter of the United States of America's presidency. Some prophets were bold to declare that President Donald Trump will win the election and were later attacked by many people both inside and outside the church when events did not turn out as expected.

This fiasco mostly online or on social media is one of the reasons why I have taken some time to write about who prophets are and how they operate in this book. Yet I will not go too deep into this matter of how to judge prophecies rightly or wrongly as it is not our primary focus.

For an example of a New Testament male prophet, I choose John the Baptist. According to Matthew's records of Jesus' words, John was not only affirmed as a prophet, but he was also said to be the greatest among prophets. I believe this is enough reason for me to choose him as a New Testament reference.

> *9 But what did you go out to see? A prophet? Yes, I say to you, and more than a prophet. 10 For this is he of whom it is written: 'Behold, I send My messenger before Your face, Who will prepare Your way before You.' 11 "Assuredly, I say to you, among those born of women there has not risen one greater than John the Baptist; but he who is least in the kingdom of heaven is greater than he.*
>
> Matthew 11:9-11

I believe Jesus said John was the greatest prophet among all the prophets before and in his days because all the others prophesied about the Messiah's coming and redemption for humanity, but John was the only one who witnessed it. Many of the other prophets were spokesmen for God declaring what they probably could not fully comprehend while John lived through the reality of his prophecy. He saw and touched Jesus, and God confirmed to him that Jesus is the Messiah he (John) was raised to announce his coming and most importantly, he witnessed Jesus in action living and demonstrating the reality of the kingdom of God.

> *In those days John the Baptist came preaching in the wilderness of Judea, ² and saying, "Repent, for the kingdom of heaven is at hand!" ³ For this is he who was spoken of by the prophet Isaiah, saying: "The voice of one crying in the wilderness: 'Prepare the way of the LORD; Make His paths straight."*
>
> Matthew 3:1-3

Let me highlight how John functioned as a prophet.
- John was divinely graced to hear messages from God.
- John was a spokesman for God, declaring the coming of the Messiah and the kingdom of God.

John, like many other Old Testament prophets, declared what God was planning to do for Israel and hence called them to repent of their wicked ways. Yet John's ministry as a prophet was different in that he did not declare God's impending judgment over the people or declare curses or the wrath of God that would come upon them if they rebelled. That was the major difference between Old Testament and New Testament prophets. Although New Testament prophets can be spokesmen and seers, they tend to bring words of edification, comfort and foretell God's heart concerning future events.

> *² For he who speaks in a tongue does not speak to men*

but to God, for no one understands him; however, in the spirit he speaks mysteries. ³ But he who prophesies speaks edification and exhortation and comfort to men.

1 Corinthians 14:2-3

There are other differences, but I will not discuss them at this point as this chapter is to give you a basic understanding of the office of the prophet.

Moses The Prophet

As mentioned earlier one bible character that many Christians are familiar with is Moses. Everyone who attended Sunday school must have heard Moses' story at least once. He was popularly known as the leader raised by God to be Israel's deliverer. I will admit that I also did not notice his call to the office of a prophet for a long time because I focused more on God referring to his brother Aaron as a prophet.

*So, the LORD said to Moses: "See, I have made you as God to Pharaoh, and Aaron your brother shall **be your prophet**. ² You shall speak all that I command you. And Aaron your brother shall tell Pharaoh to send the children of Israel out of his land.*

Exodus 7:1-2

A closer look at the text helped me learn that though the

word prophet 'nabi' was used for Aaron, it was to indicate that he was chosen as a spokesman for Moses. Note that God insisted that Moses was still the one who will be His spokesman. Moses could not get out of being the prophet God was calling him to be even with his excuses about stuttering and lack of eloquence. Even after reading the third and fourth chapters of Exodus where God called Moses several times, it still did not sink in that Moses held the office of a prophet, as such, I missed seeing that he functioned as a prophet of God to Pharaoh, the Egyptians, and His people.

> ¹⁵ Moreover God said to Moses, "Thus you shall **say to the children of Israel**: 'The LORD God of your fathers, the God of Abraham, the God of Isaac, and the God of Jacob, has sent me to you. This is My name forever, and this is My memorial to all generations.' ¹⁶ Go and gather the elders of Israel together, and say to them, 'The LORD God of your fathers, the God of Abraham, of Isaac, and of Jacob, appeared to me, saying, "I have surely visited you and seen what is done to you in Egypt;
> ¹⁷ and I have said I will bring you up out of the affliction of Egypt to the land of the Canaanites and the Hittites and the Amorites and the Perizzites and the Hivites and the Jebusites, to a land flowing with milk and honey."' ¹⁸ Then they will heed your voice; and you shall come, you and the elders of Israel, to the king of Egypt; and you shall say to him, 'The LORD God of the Hebrews has met with

us; and now, please, let us go three days' journey into the
wilderness, that we may sacrifice to the Lord our God.'

Exodus 3:15-18

Now you can understand why I have intentionally chosen to write about Moses' ministry as a prophet as it is significant to the focus of this book. He was one prophet that not only encountered a Pharaoh but had to go into battle with him and prevailed. Let me expose a few truths to you about the prophetic ministry of Moses.

- Moses supernaturally heard the voice of God.
- Moses was anointed to be God's spokesman declaring His word to Pharaoh.
- Moses boldly came against Pharaoh and his evil plans for the Hebrews as he confronted him with God's plan for them.
- Moses was anointed to demonstrate the miracle-working power of God, thus showing God's superiority.
- Moses prevailed over Pharaoh.

In a later chapter, I write more about the confrontations between Moses and Pharaoh. There you will learn more about the importance of prophets in God's plans to divinely intervene when there is injustice in the earth.

The 2st Century Prophets

Many people today do not have much difficulty in believing

in the office and functions of the prophet in the bible, particularly the Old Testament. Their difficulty shows up when it concerns accepting that the office and function of the prophet are still in operation today. This is primarily because of an erroneous doctrine that crept into the body of Christ popularly known as the 'cessation doctrine' or 'cessationism' which is a Protestant doctrine that says spiritual gifts such as speaking in tongues, prophecy and healing ceased with the Apostolic Age. Reformers such as John Calvin originated this view, consequently, some Christians believe that there are no prophets in the 21st century and they are far from the truth.

One way God has helped me to deal with arguments relating to the cessation of any concept or ordinance that the bible shows was established by God is to go back to review God's original plan for establishing it.

> ...Some Christians believe that there are no prophets in the 21st century...

Clearly from the Old Testament, we can deduce that God raised prophets because he needed men that will be anointed to hear His voice, see into the spirit realm and ultimately be spokespeople for Him. This tells me that God cares about ensuring that His children are not in the dark or ignorant of what He is doing and wants to do in the future.

In the New Testament, Apostle Paul was inspired to write to the Ephesian Church about the five major offices that God established to help His children grow and fulfil their ministry.

One of those offices is that of the prophet.

> *[11] And He Himself gave some to be apostles, some prophets, some evangelists, and some pastors and teachers, [12] for the equipping of the saints for the work of ministry, for the [a]edifying of the body of Christ,*
>
> Ephesians 4:11-12

The word prophet here is the Greek word 'prophetes' which means interpreter of oracles or other hidden things, a spokesman as well as one inspired to declare future events as it relates to the kingdom of God. I will summarise the meaning of the word ''prophetes' as one anointed with divine eyesight, insight, and foresight.

To have divine eyesight is to be anointed by God to hear and see into the realm of the spirit, accessing what should have been visible to men. While to have divine insight is to be anointed with the supernatural understanding of events taking place in the now. And lastly, to have divine foresight is to be anointed to know what will happen in the near or distant future.

When you consider what the New Testament prophet is anointed to offer to the body of Christ, you will realise that there is no way God would have put an end to men being anointed as prophets. Those of us living in the 21st century are aware of the great level of lies and deception the kingdom of darkness has introduced into our world. Jesus forewarned us that it will get darker and darker in the last days, hence we are to be ready to shine as light. How can the body of Christ shine God's light if we lack divine eyesight, insight, and foresight?

If you remember what I shared with you in the introduction, the greatest dilemma of the events regarding the pandemic and worldwide lockdown that started in 2020 was that many including Christians did not know what was happening in the world. It was a time when the body of Christ needed prophets to speak up, I needed to hear from prophets too as an apostolic leader that was also serving as a pastor.

> To have divine eyesight is to be anointed by God to hear and see into the realm of the spirit...

So, the question of whether we need the 21st-century prophet has a clear answer. The other question is whether the body of Christ has authentic anointed prophets which I believe she does.

In my pursuit for insight and foresight, God led me to some authentic 21st-century prophets who were truly hearing from God and declaring His word. Some of them with the seer anointing had seen that there would be an outbreak of the virus months before it happened. Others had been God's spokesmen declaring since 2019 that the year 2020 was not going to be the beginning of a new decade but that of a new era. Some even went further to prophetically declare that after 2020, our world will never be the same again.

If you noticed, I have once again intentionally chosen not

to mention the names of any of these 21st-century prophets because I feel led to do so, just as I have been led not to mention the names of any 21st century Pharaohs. I trust that the Spirit of the Lord himself will lead you to discover them.

One other thing I know the Lord told me was that what many began to call a plague in 2020 was a means for God to display His power as another showdown between the Prophets and the Pharaohs begin. Like in the days of Moses, the plagues were weapons in God's hand as His prophet battled with the Pharaoh as it is today.

Prayer:

Father, I repent of my ignorance concerning the office and function of prophets. I repent for any wrong words I have spoken concerning your prophets. Please forgive me.

I thank you for the understanding I have received and pray that you will use me to bring understanding to others.

Today I pray that the ministry of the prophet will impact my life, my church and my world positively for you in Jesus' name. Amen!

CHAPTER 3

THE PLAGUES

"¹⁷ But the LORD plagued Pharaoh and his house with great plagues because of Sarai, Abram's wife. ¹⁸ And Pharaoh called Abram and said, "What is this you have done to me? Why did you not tell me that she was your wife?"

Genesis 12:17-18

What Are Plagues

Plagues played a significant role in Moses' battle with Pharaoh in Bible times and still does today which is why it is noteworthy of our discussion in this chapter as you will see. First, we turn to the dictionary for meaning, "what is a plague?" According to Webster, a plague can be defined as a disastrous evil or affliction, an epidemic disease causing a high rate of mortality or a virulent contagious febrile disease that is caused by a bacterium (Yersinia Pestis) and that occurs in bubonic, pneumonic, and septicaemic forms.

Types of Plagues

Just as there are different definitions of plague, I want you to know that it comes from different root Hebrew words and hence has different meanings each time it occurs. You will need to read the story or context where it is used for accurate understanding.

For example, the first time it is used in Genesis chapter twelve, the root word 'Nega' applies which means 'stroke or wound or disease or a mark', (e.g., leprosy).

This means that the Pharaoh and his household experienced some diseases that could also include having marks on their body before he cried out and somehow got the revelation from God about the cause of their affliction.

In Exodus where we read the account of the battle between Moses and Pharaoh, the word plague occurs many times as it was God's weapon of warfare to punish this Pharaoh and the Egyptians.

[13] Then the LORD said to Moses, "Rise early in the morning and stand before Pharaoh, and say to him, 'Thus says the LORD God of the Hebrews: "Let My people go, that they may serve Me, [14] for at this time I will send all My plagues

to your very heart, and on your servants and on your
people, that you may know that there is none like Me in
all the earth. ¹⁵ *Now if I had stretched out My hand and*
struck you and your people with pestilence, then you
would have been cut off from the earth.

Exodus 9:13-15

In the above text, the word interpreted as 'plague' is the Hebrew word 'Magepa' which could mean 'blow (fatal stroke) or slaughter (of battle) or pestilence (divine judgment)'. God was making it clear to Moses that Pharaoh and Egypt were about to be hit with a fatal blow that will lead to slaughter on a proportion that will get their attention and change Pharaoh's stony heart.

I also discovered another Hebrew word 'Maka' that was translated to the word plague. It was first used in the book of Leviticus when God was warning the children of Israel about the consequence of rebellion against him.

²¹ *'Then, if you walk contrary to Me, and are not willing*
to obey Me, I will bring on you seven times more plagues,
according to your sins.

Leviticus 26:21

The word could mean 'beating, scourging, wound or defeat'. I noticed that God was teaching his children that rebellion against him can reduce them to the same status

49

as nations like Egypt deserving punishment. In this chapter, we will focus more on the plagues that manifested between Moses' (the Prophet) battle with the Pharaoh and in the next chapter, I will share more about the battle. But first, let us get a better understanding of the sources of plagues and why God sometimes uses plagues.

Who Sends Plagues

> God was directly involved with all the initial records of the release of plagues upon men.

Plagues can come from three main sources. They can come from God, the devil and his evil cohorts, or from men. First, I will start with plagues sent by God. A close study of the Bible will reveal that God was directly involved with all the initial records of the release of plagues upon men. As said earlier, the first record of that word was in the story of the first Pharaoh in Abram's time.

> But the **LORD plagued Pharaoh** and his house with great plagues because of Sarai, Abram's wife.
> Genesis 12:17

The plague this Pharaoh suffered and every other one he and the rest of the Egyptians witnessed at the hands of Moses was brought upon him by God. There are more stories of plagues sent by God, and if you ask me, I'll say God is the best and the worst source of plagues.

It sounds contradictory, but it is not, because, if God sends a plague, then it means that He has the power to easily stop it at will. Also, if God sends a plague, no man, force or devil can stop it, a hard truth that the Pharaoh's magicians discovered too late.

> **God is the best and the worst source of plagues.**

The second source of plagues is through the devil and his evil cohorts. One bible story that reveals the devil's ability to send plagues is found in the book of Job. After getting God's permission to do something that could affect Job's body, the devil sent a horrible plague upon his body.

> *4 So Satan answered the LORD and said, "Skin for skin! Yes, all that a man has he will give for his life. 5 But stretch out Your hand now, and touch his bone and his flesh, and he will surely [b]curse You to Your face!" 6 And the LORD said to Satan, "Behold, he is in your hand, but spare his life." 7 So Satan went out from the presence of the LORD, and struck Job with painful boils from the sole of his foot to the crown of his head.*
>
> *Job 2:4-7*

It is noteworthy that the devil could not send this plague upon Job without God's permission which proves that God's

51

covenant children are supposed to be protected from plagues sent by the devil or his cohorts. Not knowing this truth is the reason why covenant children are frightened like unbelievers when there is news about a plague or epidemic.

The 2020 virus outbreak truly revealed that many of God's children either did not know this truth or did not believe it.

The second thing I want you to know about plagues sent by the devil is that God can stop it whenever He pleases as seen in Job's life where God healed him from the plague as soon as He was ready to do so and the devil could not do anything about it. In fact, there is no record of the devil ever attempting to send another plague upon Job's body.

The third possible source of plagues is men. I have deliberately decided to write more about this third source because it gives credence to the main purpose behind this book which is to expose the wickedness that exists in our world today. Our world has always had men that yield their hearts to the devil who turns them into instruments of wickedness.

For example, the bible revealed that the Pharaoh in Moses story had magicians who could turn water into blood. The ability to perform such an act means they could have poisoned the water in the past and easily caused a plague if they wanted.

> [20] *And Moses and Aaron did so, just as the LORD commanded. So he lifted up the rod and struck the waters that were in the river, in the sight of Pharaoh*

and in the sight of his servants. And all the waters that were in the river were turned to blood. ²¹ The fish that were in the river died, the river stank, and the Egyptians could not drink the water of the river. So there was blood throughout all the land of Egypt.

²² Then the magicians of Egypt did so with their enchantments; and Pharaoh's heart grew hard, and he did not heed them, as the LORD had said.

Exodus 7:20-22

Men out of deliberate rebellion against God have invited plagues upon themselves and their people. Hence wicked leaders can cause their subjects to suffer plagues by provoking God's judgment. Christians should endeavour to discern the spirit leading those they elect as national leaders. Solomon gave us a warning concerning this matter.

> Modern history also reveals that men create plagues and release them to harm other people

*When the righteous are in authority, the people rejoice;
But when a wicked man rules, the people groan*

Proverbs 29:2

Modern history also reveals that men create plagues and release them to harm other people as they please. Infectious diseases had potential impact on people and armies as early as

53

600 B.C. The crude use of filth and cadavers, animal carcasses, and contagion had devastating effects and weakened the enemy. Also polluting the opposing army's wells and water sources was a common strategy that continued to be used through the many European wars, the American Civil War, and even into the 20th century.

One of the first recorded use of biological warfare occurred in 1347, when Mongol forces were reported to have catapulted plague-infested bodies over the walls into the Black Sea port of Caffa (now Feodosiya, Ukraine) which was at that time a Genoese trade centre in the Crimean Peninsula.

Some historians believe that ships from the besieged city returned to Italy with the plague, starting the Black Death pandemic that swept through Europe over the next four years and killed some twenty-five million people (about one-third of the population). Another disease that has been used as an effective biological weapon in The New World is smallpox.

Pizarro is said to have presented South American natives with variola-contaminated clothing in the 15th century. Also, during the French-Indian War (1754–1767), Sir Jeffrey Amherst, the commander of the British forces in North America, suggested the deliberate use of smallpox to diminish the native Indian population hostile to the British. (see reference at the end.)

Many countries were known to have worked on developing biological weapons to create plagues in enemy nations during the first and second world wars. And in the years immediately after World War II, newspapers were filled with articles about disease outbreaks caused by foreign agents armed with biological weapons.

Also, during the Korean War, the Soviet Union, China, and North Korea accused the USA of using agents of biological warfare against North Korea. Years later, the USA admitted that it had the capacity to produce such weapons, although it denied using them.

There are speculations about the origin of the recent COVID-19 virus outbreak. Investigative reports by some well-known media houses have claimed that the virus escaped from the Wuhan Institute of Virology (WIV) laboratories. There are further claims that the WIV was commissioned by the US National Institute of Health (NIH) around 2017 to conduct gain-of-function research work on the SARS-CoV-2 coronavirus.

Many believe that these research laboratories were the source of the outbreak. Whether this is true or not, I cannot authoritatively confirm at this point, but I strongly suspect that the COVID-19 plague was man-made. I believe there are enough wicked and devilish people on earth that would desire to use this plague to achieve their selfish and demonic agendas.

It is interesting to note how some of the movers and shakers of our world (Pharaohs) immediately swung into action to profit and advance their agendas as soon as the outbreak was promoted to pandemic status by the World

PHARAOHS, PROPHETS & PLAGUES

Health Organization (WHO). Someday the truth will be revealed about the shady secrets they are hiding from the world.

I am convinced that the wicked are currently calling what is the truth a conspiracy theory to further deceive many. What the liars and deceivers forget is that there is a God in heaven who knows and can use all things including the plagues for His glory.

Why God Uses Plagues

I did some intensive study on this matter of plagues in the bible and discovered that God is responsible for its occurrence in most cases. From Genesis to Revelation, we read of Him sending plagues or threatening to send one. In every case, you will notice that God primarily uses this threat to warn his children about their rebellion and unrepentant sinful nature. And when He sends a plague to a people or land, it is to punish them for their continuous rebellion and unwillingness to repent.

So, we can easily conclude that plagues are used by God to get men to repent and turn from our wicked ways. Unfortunately, we tend to go back to our sinful ways which keep attracting God's judgment.

Making the Best Use of Plagues

A wise leader once said, "never let a good crisis go to waste". At first, I was a bit confused about what he was trying to say.

Then he explained that we must always try to learn as much as we can from every crisis so we do not find ourselves in the same crisis in the future and if we do, we will know how to better deal with it. With this thought in mind, I believe that God expects us to learn lessons from plagues so that we do not go back to doing what brought the plague in the past. Unfortunately, we do not learn from the past and hence keep attracting God's judgments like plagues.

If Israel had learnt from what they saw the Egyptians go through, they would not have built and worshipped a golden calf in the wilderness. Even if we make the excuse that Moses was yet to give them the ten commandments and they did not know that

> "...Never let a good crisis go to waste".

it was wrong to worship a graven image, Israel had many instances in their future where they went back to repeat the same rebellious act. The books of Kings and Chronicles are filled with stories of Israel's continuous rebellion against God that attracted plagues on them.

One of the best insights I got during the 2020 global pandemic was from a dear friend and man of God, Ade Omooba MBE who is pastor and co-founder of Christian Concern UK. During a conversation in the middle of the lockdown, he explained how in prayer during the outbreak, he had asked God to blow away the virus.

What he heard from God in response was not what he expected which prompted him to change his prayer focus. He went on to tell me that he ended up asking the Lord to please help us learn every lesson that we ought to learn before He takes away the plague.

Prayer:

Father, in Jesus' name, I thank you for a better understanding of plagues and why you send or permit them.

I repent from all my past sins and rebellion against you that may have opened me up for judgment with a plague.

I also ask for forgiveness on behalf of my country, for every sin that could have opened us up to the global pandemic.

Please make me a voice for righteousness and one that will bring your blessing upon your people and not a curse.

I ask for all these in the precious name of Jesus Christ. Amen!

CHAPTER 4

OVERCOMING FEAR

"For God has not given us a spirit of fear, but of power and of love and of a sound mind.

2 Timothy 1:7

ONE PHRASE USED TO define fear that has become a revelatory truth for me is "False Evidence Appearing Real". Fear can easily become one of the greatest challenges in the life of a child of God. This is because it has the potential to distort truth such that you begin to experience negative emotions about a matter that does not exist. It also has the potential to directly oppose faith which is the most important ingredient that should be present in the life of every child of God.

What is Fear?

Fear is a major weapon in the devil's arsenal, and he has been using it against men from the beginning of time. Fear is important to understanding the contention between Pharaohs and Prophets, more so about plagues which is why we want to uncover its shades in this chapter. Once again, I want to remind you that during the 2020 pandemic, the fear of death filled the world which led to the global lockdown aided by exaggerations from media outlets.

Even Israel, inhabited by some of the most religious people on earth was on total lockdown. It was during the Passover in April 2020 it dawned on me that Israel was celebrating Passover in total lockdown for the second time since God instructed them to stay indoors the day before the spirit of death was to Passover Egypt. This revelation further reinforced the fact that we were experiencing events of historical proportions.

> Fear is a major weapon in the devil's arsenal...

During this time, it also became evident that many Christians were gripped by fear, I remember that the first message the Lord gave me to preach to my congregation and all the people within our ministry's reach was about understanding and overcoming fear. That message became the foundation to messages about Pharaohs and Prophets that were to follow as led by the Spirit of God.

Webster's dictionary defines fear as "an unpleasant often strong emotion caused by anticipation or awareness of danger". Take note of the following truths from this definition:

- Fear is an emotion.
- Fear anticipates danger.
- Fear anticipates a negative future outcome.

I chose to highlight this definition as it is the closest I could find about the original Hebrew word translated to fear. The word 'fear' occurs over five hundred times in the King James Bible. See how 'fear' or the verb form 'afraid' is used the first time according to the King James bible.

"After these things the word of the LORD came unto Abram in a vision, saying, Fear not, Abram: I am thy shield, and thy exceeding great reward."

Genesis 15:1

Another word that translates to fear in English is the Hebrew word 'yare' which means to revere or stand in awe. This is the word used many times in the Old Testament when the word of God is encouraging us to fear God. Other Hebrew words translated to fear are as follows:

- 'yira' meaning terror or a terrifying thing (Genesis 20:11).
- 'pahad' meaning terror or dread (Genesis 31:42).
- 'ema' meaning dread, terror, or horror (Exodus 15:12).

My investigation revealed that the last word 'ema' which means terror and horror was the most used in the story of Moses' battle with Pharaoh. God was letting us know what kind of fear the Egyptians were to experience. They were to anticipate horror because of God's intervention on behalf of His Hebrew children.

Fear Is A Spirit

It is important that you understand that fear is not just an emotion, but it is also a spirit. I mean that there are satanic spirits called fear whose primary assignment is to attack the heart and minds of man to provoke the anticipation of danger and negative outcomes. Let me take you back to the bible text highlighted at the beginning of this chapter.

> *"For God has not given us a spirit of fear, but of power and of love and of a sound mind.*
>
> 2 Timothy 1:7

You need to understand that fear is not just an emotion, but also a spirit. I mean that there are demonic spirits called fear whose primary assignment is to attack the heart and minds of men to provoke the anticipation of danger and negative outcomes.

In the scripture above, Paul was teaching his spiritual son Timothy to not entertain fear of any opposition to his ministerial assignment. In doing this, he reveals to Timothy that fear is a spirit that possesses the ability to contend with our faith in the love of God and the power of God. Fear can also deny us of having a sound mind, a revelation that should help us discern that some of the emotions we experience are not natural but demonically induced.

Certain areas of captivity suffered by mankind are only possible because of ignorance of the spiritual forces in operation. Fear has the power to cripple and hence rob you of the life and future God preordained for you. These spirits of fear are used by the devil to negate your faith in God. Here are a few of the different manifestations of the spirit of fear and its effects.

> ...These spirits of fear are used by the devil to negate your faith in God.

Fear of evil happening to you: This is when a person is constantly bombarded with emotions and anticipation of something bad happening to them. This is common with parents who constantly fear that something bad will happen to their child. Unfortunately, some may end up attracting what they fear the most like Job.

"For the thing I greatly feared has come upon me.
Job 3:25.*"*

Fear of adverse circumstances: This emotion has to do with anticipating negative events or outcomes. A good example is that of a person anticipating that they will run out of money. Such a person becomes stingy and even disobedient to God's command to give. Solomon has a word of wisdom for such people.

> *"He who observes the wind will not sow, and he who regards the clouds will not reap".*
>
> Ecclesiastes 11:4

Fear of failure: This is the emotion of anticipating that anything you embark upon will fail. This fear stops many people from even trying, as a result, many of God's children are unwilling to pursue the career or business idea or ministry that God has called them into. Remember Moses' initial response when God called him to go face Pharaoh and get the children of Israel out of Egypt. Moses gave every excuse he could find including the fact that he was not eloquent. He was afraid he would fail with the assignment God was giving him.

> *¹⁰ Then Moses said to the LORD, "O my Lord, I am not eloquent, neither before nor since You have spoken to Your servant; but I am slow of speech and slow of tongue."*
>
> Exodus 4:10

People permit many fears in their lives that cripple them because of the overwhelming emotions that something negative is about to happen to them. As of the time of writing this book, many people are still gripped by the fear of dying from the coronavirus. There is no better time for the children of God to teach and preach faith in God than now. We must let the world know that what God has made available for His children is the spirit of love, power and a sound mind.

Faith Over Fear

Fear works like faith. If faith is the magnetic force that attracts positive outcomes, fear is the magnetic force that attracts negative outcomes. Like I wrote earlier, one fear that Job entertained in his heart was that His children may come under God's judgment and be killed because of their sin.

> ...Fear is the magnetic force that attracts negative outcomes.

For this reason, he continually made sacrifices on their behalf, soon, what he feared the most happened. The antidote to suffering from the emotions of fear is to develop your faith.

Experiencing peace does not necessarily mean the absence of trouble or crisis but rather the presence of calmness and confidence that all will be well even amidst the trouble or crisis.

You must learn to develop your faith in God that all will be well to the extent that it is difficult for any foul spirit of fear to get you to anticipate danger and negative outcomes. I call this "faith over fear".

PHARAOHS, PROPHETS & PLAGUES

A careful study of the encounter Moses had with God in Exodus three and four reveals that Moses was afraid to accept God's assignment for him.

He was called by God to be an Apostle (an emissary or a sent one) and a Prophet (a spokesman) for God but it was too much for a man who tried to be a deliverer and failed forty years earlier.

God knew that the only way He would get Moses to accept this assignment was to take time to build Moses' faith in Him.

God had to demonstrate the superiority of His power and authority to whatever Pharaoh will have to offer. This is primarily why God began to work miracles for Moses to see and experience.

One of the challenges of the 21st-century church is that some denominations have rejected the truth that God still works miracles and as a result have fewer tools to build the faith of their people in God.

The believers who were taught that the gift of healings have ceased with the early apostle were the most petrified when the virus outbreak started. Let's take a look at some of the miracles God performed to build Moses' faith.

God turned Moses' rod into a serpent

² *So the Lord said to him, "What is that in your hand?"*
He said, "A rod."

³ And He said, "Cast it on the ground." So he cast it on the ground, and it became a serpent; and Moses fled from it. ⁴ Then the Lord said to Moses, "Reach out your hand and take it by the tail" (and he reached out his hand and caught it, and it became a rod in his hand)

Exodus 4:2-4

Notice that not only did God prove that He could turn a non-living thing into a living thing, but He also showed that He was able to turn a living thing back to a non-living thing. In asking Moses to pick up the serpent, God also managed to break Moses' fear of the serpent.

I want to believe you know that the serpent represented the devil and all his power to strike and kill Moses with his venom.

God caused Moses hand to become leprous

⁶ Furthermore the Lord said to him, "Now put your hand in your bosom." And he put his hand in his bosom, and when he took it out, behold, his hand was leprous, like snow. ⁷ And He said, "Put your hand in your bosom again." So he put his hand in his bosom again, and drew it out of his bosom, and behold, it was restored like his other flesh.

Exodus 4:6-7

By doing this God proved to Moses that He can cause infirmity and plagues to happen to a person's body and also that God can heal a person of a plague instantly. In other words,

Moses was to develop faith in the truth that while God can bring a plague upon the Egyptians, He could prevent the plague from affecting the Hebrews at the same time.

Again, it is important to note that the more your faith grows in God's ability the less you will fear the devil's. It was important for God to let Moses know that He who was on his side is greater than anything that Pharaoh and the power behind him could offer. Like Paul taught the believers in Rome while they were under Roman persecution, if God is for them, no one could prevail against them.

> ...The more your faith grows in God's ability the less you will fear the devil's.

31 What then shall we say to these things? If God is for us, who can be against us?

Romans 8:31

The Power of the Revelation of Love

By now, it should be clear to you that God does not desire that any of His children live in fear because fear leads to doubt and unbelief which displeases God.

⁶ But without faith it is impossible to please Him, for he who comes to God must believe that He is, and that He is a rewarder of those who diligently seek Him.

Hebrews 11:6

The writer of Hebrews made it clear that our faith pleases God and that anyone that must come to God must know Him for who He is. Our God has many awesome qualities including faithfulness, holiness, and trustworthiness. Out of all His many qualities, the most important one that we must never forget when it comes to this subject of faith is His love for us.

God loves us much more than you and I can ever comprehend. The revelation of His love for you will cause you to be at peace in many areas of your life where you are tempted to worry or become anxious.

According to John, one of the apostles of Jesus Christ, a revelation of the perfect love of God will demolish whatever the spirit of fear has been assigned to do in your heart.

¹⁷ Love has been perfected among us in this: that we may have boldness in the day of judgment; because as He is, so are we in this world. ¹⁸ There is no fear in love; but perfect love casts out fear, because fear involves torment. But he who fears has not been made perfect in love. 19 We love Him because He first loved us.

1 John 4:17-19

69

This makes it clear that God's children who believe in the love of God towards us should not be prone to fear like unbelievers who are yet to know Him.

Another eyeopener for me during the pandemic about the level of fear among Christians is that many of us are yet to come to the revelation of the perfect love of God.

Notice that in the text I have just shared with you, John highlighted that believers were not to fear even death itself as the love of the Father promises that it will be well with us on judgment day.

I was shocked to see many church leaders demonstrate fear of death during the lockdown. Many hid at home for months, only communicating and preaching to their congregants via various internet technologies even when the government had permitted church gatherings. I saw a lot of this in the UK where I live.

Faith as A Lifestyle

All children of God are called to a life of faith. We are to walk by faith daily with the understanding that "fear permitted is faith contaminated". There are four different places in both the Old and New Testament where God makes it clear that all those who have been redeemed, justified, and made righteous are to have a lifestyle of faith.

*Behold the proud, His soul is not upright in him; But **the just shall live by his faith.***

Habakkuk 2:4

*For in it the righteousness of God is revealed from faith to faith; as it is written, **"The just shall live by faith."***

Romans 1:17

*But that no one is justified by the law in the sight of God is evident, for **"the just shall live by faith."***

Galatians 3:11

*Now **the just shall live by faith**; But if anyone draws back, My soul has no pleasure in him.*

Hebrews 10:38

With these four portions of scriptures from three different witnesses namely Habakkuk, Apostle Paul, and the writer of the book of Hebrew, (Habakkuk 2:4, Romans 1:17, Galatians 3:11, Hebrews 10:38) we can indeed conclude that God wants us to live by faith daily. So, then what must you do to ensure that the enemy does not get you to live in fear? I will give you a couple of tips.

Guard your heart and mind diligently: Every battle is won or lost in the mind. Fear is introduced to your mind in the form of negative information through your eye or ear gate.

Intentionally make a paradigm shift: Introduce new thoughts to eliminate old ones. Deliberately remind yourself of the past victories and breakthroughs God gave you. Train yourself to believe that if God did it once before, He can do it again.

Remember that I mentioned earlier that during the 2020 virus outbreak, many Christians were overwhelmed by fear. This was primarily because we were all bombarded by negative news of people dying on most media. I also mentioned that I started to teach my congregation about overcoming this fear. Here are some of the spiritual nuggets I dropped in their hearts:

> Train yourself to believe that if God did it once before, He can do it again.

Viruses are nothing new. God used them as part of plagues (pestilence and boils) in Egypt –Exodus:9.

There is nothing new about this adversity and God will get you through it –1 Corinthians 10:13.

Coronavirus is just another name and hence is subject to the name of Jesus – Philippians 2:9-11.

Maintain the right revelation of God in your heart and let your confession line up with the truth in your heart –1 John 4:18.

Prayer:

Heavenly Father, I thank you for the truth I have just learnt about fear. I repent for living in fear. Today, I reject the spirit of fear and embrace the spirit of love, power and a sound mind. Please strengthen my faith in you and teach me how to walk by faith every day of my life in Jesus' name. Amen.

CHAPTER 5

DEFEATING THE PHAROAHS

"¹⁹ But I am sure that the king of Egypt will not let you go, no, not even by a mighty hand. ²⁰ So I will stretch out My hand and strike Egypt with all My wonders which I will do in its midst; and after that he will let you go."

Exodus 3:19-20

We have reached the point where it gets extremely exciting. This is the point where we get to review the battle between the Pharaoh and the Prophet in great depth. The words God spoke to Moses made it clear that Pharaoh was not going to be a pushover but rather a fighter, so Moses was to prepare for a major showdown. There will be major contention God said, but you Moses will prevail. In God's own words, "I will stretch my hands and strike Egypt with all my wonders", (Exodus 3:20). This was to give Moses confidence that the battle is not His but God's and all he had to do was to stand in faith.

Today many of God's covenant children shake and cry in the face of opposition. One primary reason for this is that we do not know whether God will back us up, while another is that many times, we do not understand God's weapons of warfare. Moses could not have imagined that God was going to use plagues as a weapon of warfare.

Later, I will reveal to you why I believe the 2020 virus outbreak was permitted by God and was designed to be a tool for Him to fulfil His purpose in the earth and the lives of His children. But before we get into that, I want to first help you see what and whom each party in this battle was depending on.

Understanding the Gods of the Egyptians

The story of Moses and Pharaoh's battle made it clear whom Moses was depending on for victory but not Pharaoh. Let me show you more depth about the gods that Pharaoh believed in before he had this encounter with God's prophet.

First let me start by stating that all people and nations on the earth in bible days, particularly under the Old Testament had gods they believed in. Except for the Hebrews who later became Israel, most other nations had to find a god to believe in and Egypt was no exception. Below is a list of the ten most popular gods the Egyptians worshipped during the time of this story.

1. Hapi—Egyptian god of the Nile: This Egyptian god was a water bearer.
2. Heket—Egyptian goddess of fertility, water, renewal: Heket the Egyptian goddess, had the head of a frog.
3. Geb—Egyptian god of the earth: The Egyptian god Geb was over the dust of the earth.
4. Khepri—Egyptian god of creation, movement of the sun, rebirth: Khepri the Egyptian god had the head of a fly.
5. Hathor—Egyptian goddess of love and protection: Hathor was usually depicted with the head of a cow.
6. Isis—Egyptian goddess of medicine and peace.
7. Nut—Egyptian goddess of the sky.
8. Seth—Egyptian god of storms, disorder, violence, and foreigners.
9. Ra—The sun god.
10. Pharaoh—The ultimate god of Egypt.

> Egyptians worshipped a man (Pharaoh) as their god.

I want to highlight the fact that Egyptians worshipped a man (Pharaoh) as their god. This was one of the reasons why Pharaoh felt the need to contend with Moses until it was revealed to him that his powers were inferior to that of Moses' God whose name is Jehovah.

Understanding Jehovah God

One aspect of the encounter Moses had during the burning bush incident was a proper introduction to the Almighty God. First, God introduced Himself as the God of his fathers, Abraham, Isaac, and Jacob. Moses would have heard some stories passed down from the previous generations about these fathers, yet he struggled as he could not comprehend God, considering the slavery and oppression of the Hebrews he had witnessed in Egypt. So, he inquired further.

> [13] *Then Moses said to God, "Indeed, when I come to the children of Israel and say to them, 'The God of your fathers has sent me to you,' and they say to me, 'What is His name?' what shall I say to them?"*
> [14] *And God said to Moses, "I AM WHO I AM." And He said, "Thus you shall say to the children of Israel, 'I AM has sent me to you.'"*
>
> Exodus 3:13-14

God introduced Himself as "I am who I am". Honestly, I am not sure if this helped Moses much. Today we have been granted insight to know that God was saying that He is the Almighty God who WAS and IS and IS TO COME. Also, that He is above all gods and that no other god can be compared with Him. He can be what you want Him to be, meaning He would manifest Himself to you to the level of your faith. This is still true today as it was in the days of Moses.

The major challenge with Moses understanding God in his day is the same as what many of us today struggle with. We only know and understand God to the level of our experience of Him. Moses had heard stories about God but his experience as a Hebrew was a contradiction. God had to give Moses experiences to help him know Him. I believe this was why this conversation about how to introduce God to the elders led to God manifesting miracles.

I ask you, my beloved reader, "Do you know God? Do you understand Him? How much?" I want you to understand that you must also endeavour to have encounters with God to better understand Him. I believe that Moses' understanding of God changed with each experience he had when he got back to Egypt. God would have been greater in Moses' eyes and heart with every miracle and plagues that the Egyptians suffered.

He would have learnt first-hand about the superiority of God's power and authority to whatever existed in Egypt and the Pharaoh. A careful study of Exodus will reveal that Moses became exceptionally bold when addressing Pharaoh.

> [24] *Then Pharaoh called to Moses and said, "Go, serve the LORD; only let your flocks and your herds be kept back. Let your little ones also go with you."*
> [25] *But Moses said, "You must also give us sacrifices and*

burnt offerings, that we may sacrifice to the LORD our God. ²⁶ Our livestock also shall go with us; not a hoof shall be left behind. For we must take some of them to serve the LORD our God, and even we do not know with what we must serve the LORD until we arrive there."

Exodus 10:24-26

It is interesting to see that the same Moses who was scared to face Pharaoh was giving him an offer he couldn't refuse like a Mafia boss. I pray that you and I come to the full understanding of who Jehovah is.

Demonstration of Kingdom Power and Authority

Whenever two people or powers clash, each party aims to show that they are superior in power or authority. It is not different from the battle between Moses and Pharaoh. Pharaoh flexed his muscles till the last day when it dawned on him that he was no match for the prophet of God.

Like I said in the earlier chapters, today in the 21st century, we still have pharaohs and prophets. These pharaohs are displaying their incredible power and authority which comes from the incredible wealth and influence they have amassed. The challenge is that they do not know God nor regard His prophets. Unless the prophets rise to fight, the pharaohs will continue to dominate our world.

The 21st-century prophets must be willing to rise, speak

up and fight as Moses did in his time. I believe with all my heart that the 2020 pandemic can be likened to a plague and hence another opportunity for God to show forth His glory and power as He did in Moses' days.

My in-depth study into the plagues suffered by Egypt revealed that with each plague, God was deliberately exposing an Egyptian god and their inferior powers in comparison to Himself.

Let us take a closer look at the Egyptian gods I listed earlier and the ten plagues.

Hapi—Egyptian god of the Nile, he was a water bearer.
The first plague the Egyptians received from God was that of turning their water to blood. Consequently, all the fish died, the river stank, but the god 'Hapi' could not purify the water and bring the fishes back to life. Though Pharaoh's demonic magicians could turn water to blood, they could not reverse what the prophet Moses had done.

Heket—Egyptian goddess of fertility, water, renewal, she had the head of a frog.
The second plague was of frogs that came up from the river and were in their houses, in their food, in their clothing, and every place possible. Only Moses was able to make the frogs go away revealing that 'Heket' was powerless.
Geb—Egyptian god of the earth, he was over the dust of the earth.

The third plague involved turning dust into lice throughout the land, on both people and beasts. 'Geb' who was worshipped as the god of dust could not do anything to fix the plague.

Khepri—Egyptian God of creation, movement of the sun, rebirth, he had the head of a fly.
The fourth Egyptian plague, which consisted of flies, began the great miracle of separation where the plagues only affected the Egyptians while the Hebrews remained unscathed. Again, the god 'Khepri' that they worshipped was not able to help them.

Hathor—Egyptian goddess of love and protection, she was usually depicted with the head of a cow.
The fifth plague brought about the death of cattle and livestock. This plague affected the Egyptians creating a huge economic disaster in the areas of food, transportation, military supplies, farming, and economic goods that were produced by these livestock. Guess what? 'Hathor' could not protect their livestock.

Isis—Egyptian goddess of medicine and peace
The sixth plague involved ashes turning into boils and sores on the Egyptians' body. God had taken the battle to a more personal level for the Egyptians and once again, their goddess of medicine and peace 'Isis' could not help them.

Nut—Egyptian goddess of the sky

The seventh plague rained down hails of unspeakable quantity (with the ability to destroy) from the sky which turned to fire as they hit the ground. Nut the goddess of the sky could not stop it.

Seth—Egyptian god of storms, disorder, violence, and foreigners

The eighth plague involved locusts sent as foreigners from the sky that devoured whatever was saved after the hail. The god Seth was useless against the foreigners and the disorder they created.

Ra—The sun god

The ninth plague was darkness over the land of Egypt for three days. This complete absence of light was a representation of death, judgment, and hopelessness. 'Ra' the sun god was unable to give light amid the darkness.

Pharaoh—The ultimate god of Egypt

Pharaoh the king of Egypt was worshipped by the Egyptians and was considered the greatest Egyptian god of all believed to be the son of Ra himself, manifest in the flesh. The tenth and the last plague was the death of all the firstborns of Egypt (both human and animals). Pharaoh could not save his son and thus had no choice but to surrender to the request of the prophet of God.

83

Authority to Stop Illegal Activities

One common question that people ask when evil happens in our world is "how can a good and powerful God exist but does nothing to stop evil from taking place?" I am sure you have heard some version of this question before. The bible-based answer to this is that God has given men the free will to choose between good and evil.

> Evil things do not only happen because of the existence of evil-hearted people but also because of lack of intervention by good-hearted people.

Good people do good deeds and unfortunately, some other people choose bad deeds. Evil things do not only happen because of the existence of evil-hearted people but also because of lack of intervention by good-hearted people. Sometimes good people like Christians do not understand that they have the power and authority to stop evil people from carrying out their evil deed.

A sound understanding of the power and authority available to children of God will make us understand that we do not have to spectate when the enemy and his human agents are raking havoc in our world. The Hebrews who were God's covenant children allowed Pharaohs to deal shrewdly with them because they did not know they could do something about it. Moses tried to resist the evil forty years before his burning bush encounter with God.

At that time, he did not know God nor the power and authority available through an intimate relationship with Him. It was only after his encounter with God that he too began to contend with evil people to stop their illegal activities. From the day that God heard the cry of His children in Egypt and decided to set them free, every oppressive activity by Pharaoh was illegal. Moses became the prophet of God that declared the powerful words that ended Pharaoh's wicked works.

Again, many of God's children today are permitting illegitimate activities to happen around us because we do not know the authority and power available to us. All that we need is to pursue real encounters with our all-powerful and almighty God. Then we can step up and step out like Moses.

Daniel was another prophet that knew to cry out to God to stop the illegal activities of Israel's enemy.

> [32] *Those who do wickedly against the covenant he shall]corrupt with flattery; but the people who know their God shall be strong, and carry out great exploits.* [33] *And those of the people who understand shall instruct many; yet for many days they shall fall by sword and flame, by captivity and plundering.*
>
> Daniel 11:32-33

Daniel was a man who had encountered God on many levels and thus knew what He was saying. Indeed, those who have come to know God on a personal and experiential level will be able to do great exploits including stopping the illegitimate works of the enemy.

The lack of intimate knowledge of God caused Israel to unnecessarily remain in captivity. Likewise, Jesus declared authoritatively that captivity, blindness, and bondage of God's covenant children were illegal and needed to stop when He began His ministry.

> *"The Spirit of the Lord GOD is upon Me because the LORD has anointed Me. To preach good tidings to the poor; He has sent Me to [a]heal the broken-hearted, To proclaim liberty to the captives, And the opening of the prison to those who are bound;*
>
> Isaiah 61:1

Jesus made this declaration because He knew that He had every authority to do so and that heaven will back Him up. Always remember that power can come through gifts of the spirit, but authority comes from an intimate relationship with the Father.

Prayer:

Heavenly Father, I thank you for the fresh revelation of who I am as your child and the power and authority of your kingdom.

Help me to use my mouth to speak your words like a

prophet and declare judgement over the works of the wicked.

I pray for renewed strength, grace and wisdom for a life of victory in Jesus' name. Amen.

CHAPTER 6

SUPPORTING THE PROPHETS

Then I was given a reed like a measuring rod. And the angel stood, saying, "Rise and measure the temple of God, the altar, and those who worship there. ² But leave out the court which is outside the temple, and do not measure it, for it has been given to the Gentiles. And they will tread the holy city underfoot for forty-two months. ³ And I will give power to my wo witnesses, and they will prophesy one thousand two hundred and sixty days, clothed in sackcloth."

Revelation 11:1-3

Importance of Prophets in the Last Days

An awesome privilege that our heavenly Father gave us is the ability to foresee the end of days ahead of time. I love it when preachers declare that (we) the children of God can read the end of the book (The Bible) and see that we ultimately win, of which recent years, I am becoming a student of the book of Revelation': a revelation of the end-time events given to John by God and our Lord Jesus Christ.

A careful study of the final events on earth reveals more showdowns between the saints of God and the forces of evil, namely the beast and the antichrist. In one of the major showdowns, Revelations reveals that two witnesses that will operate in the office of prophets will end up in a battle with the beast.

I discovered that the beast was another type of Pharaoh as it is also described as one with incredible power in the earth at the time spoken of. I also noticed that there are plagues involved in this battle between the prophets and this beast (or Pharaoh).

In the end, God who raised the prophets and called them into the prophetic for one thousand two hundred and sixty days was ready to back them up with His powers. Notice that these prophets could demonstrate God's power using plagues.

> [5] And if anyone wants to harm them, fire proceeds from their mouth and devours their enemies. And if anyone wants to harm them, he must be killed in this manner. [6] These have power to shut heaven, so that no rain falls in the days of their prophecy; and they have power over

waters to turn them to blood, and to strike the earth with all plagues, as often as they desire.

Revelation 11:5-6

One of the two prophets is likened to Elijah who had the power to shut up the heavens and stop the rain. The other prophet is likened to Moses with the power to turn water into blood. It is easy to conclude that prophets declaring the word of God will be needed on earth till the end of the world as we know it. This fivefold ministry cannot be allowed to disintegrate and thus believers today must continue to have faith in its existence and validity.

Stop Killing God's Prophets

One glaring thing throughout the bible is that the devil and his cohorts hate prophets. The devil hates prophets because of God's empowerment on them to see and hear from Him. He also hates that they are graced to be God's spokesmen. The devil is the prince of darkness and the power of the air. He desires to keep men in darkness as much as possible by exercising control over the airwaves and hence the information accessible to men.

Remember that the devil himself is in the dark concerning certain matters as he is not omniscient like God. He and his cohorts only know what is revealed to them when it concerns futuristic matters which is why he inspired the beast to fight with and kill the prophets mentioned in Revelation chapter eleven.

> [7] *When they finish their testimony, the beast that ascends out of the bottomless pit will make war against them, overcome them, and kill them.*
>
> Revelation 11:7

Understand that the devil has been attacking prophets from as early as the days of Abraham and Moses and the interesting thing about these attacks is that he always manages to find human agents that allow themselves to be used to attack the prophets of God. Ignorant men have been the devil's agents for killing prophets from ancient days till now. Let us look at a couple of people he used to oppose Moses.

> [20] *Then, as they came out from Pharaoh, they met Moses and Aaron who stood there to meet them.* [21] *And they said to them, "Let the LORD look on you and judge, because you have made [b]us abhorrent in the sight of Pharaoh and in the sight of his servants, to put a sword in their hand to kill us."*
>
> Exodus 5:20-21
>
> *Now Korah the son of Izhar, the son of Kohath, the son of Levi, with Dathan and Abiram the sons of Eliab, and On the son of Peleth, sons of Reuben, took men;* [2] *and they rose up before Moses with some of the children of*

*Israel, two hundred and fifty leaders of the congregation,
representatives of the congregation, men of renown. ³
They gathered together against Moses and Aaron, and
said to them, "You [a]take too much upon yourselves, for
all the congregation is holy, every one of them, and the
LORD is among them. Why then do you exalt yourselves
above the assembly of the LORD?"*

Numbers 16:1-3

Based on the scriptural references above, the first group
were the elders among the Hebrews in Egypt. They did not
know Moses as a prophet and had not yet experienced the
grace of God upon his life so, they blamed him for making
Pharaoh mad at them and were willing to discard the prophetic
word that he had given them about their freedom from Egypt
and Pharaoh.

The second passage in Numbers reveals a second group
that opposed Moses, made up of Korah, Dathan and Abiram
who were sons of Levi and some others. They were the worst
of the two groups that came against Moses because they
had at least witnessed many signs and wonders done by him.
Most importantly, they had seen many of the prophetic words
that Moses gave them come to pass including their exodus
from Egypt.

On the surface, it looked like they were only challenging
Moses' authority but with revelation from the Holy Spirit, I
realised that what they had an issue with was that Moses

operated as God's spokesman or prophet. Notice how they claimed to also be holy and hence able to hear God. The devil was using these men to challenge Moses' office and credibility as an authentic prophet of God. They would have ultimately caused the children of Israel to doubt the authenticity of the prophetic words Moses had given them.

It is possible that they attacked Moses because some things had not happened the way they thought they would and, in their timing, seeing that they were in the wilderness for much longer than any of them including Moses would have expected.

They were sons of Levi, priests, leaders, and men of renown among the people which makes it more shocking that Moses would be attacked by those who should be co-ministers with him. Unfortunately, the story hasn't changed as prophets get attacked by other ministers and Christians. It became evident to me in 2020 that the devil was at it again. There were a couple of prophecies by some prophets of God that did not pan out like some had expected which ultimately led to a massive attack against some prophets using every platform possible including social media.

The first one was about the prediction on when the COVID-19 outbreak will end. A few prophets had declared at the beginning of the year that the virus will soon disintegrate around the time of Pentecost. I believe that the initial virus outbreak was dealt with spiritually at this time because the death and hospitalization curve flattened out starting from around Passover in April.

The curve trend started heading downwards after Pentecost during the first week of June and for most people, the second wave that broke out by autumn meant that the prophets got it wrong which I do not agree with for many reasons. One of it is that I believe the second wave was a separate outbreak and not the original one that allegedly started from Wuhan, China.

The second set of prophecies that caused an even worst response has to do with the US Presidential elections. Some prophets had declared that God showed them that President Donald Trump will win the elections.

Unfortunately, the events that followed the election which I believe included a lot of dishonesty led to his opponent Joe Biden being declared as the winner. I do not think I can explain to you why I believe those prophets were not wrong in this book, however, the ones who declared that President Trump will be inaugurated on the 20th of January 2021 were wrong. It is possible to argue who won the elections and whether it was rigged or not, but it is not possible to argue who got sworn in as the forty-sixth president of the United States of America.

All I can allude to is that this incident led to a major attack against prophets. I was shocked to hear that one prophet by the name Chris Vallotton (Bethel Church, Reading CA) received death threats online. That was when it became clear that the devil was out to kill God's prophets again.

It is bad enough that many were pressured to apologise on the premise that they heard wrong but to send death threats is demonic. If a prophet has to apologise about a word, they honestly believe they heard from God, what do you think will happen to that prophet? I can liken it to committing suicide as far as their prophetic office is concerned. Can you imagine what a prophet like that will go through the next time they hear a word from God that might have the potential to cause controversy?

This reminds me of the story of Micaiah in 1 Kings chapter twenty-two, he was a prophet who heard contrary prophecies from what the other prophets heard. Four hundred prophets had given the kings of Israel and Judah the go-ahead to go to war assuring them that God had revealed that they would be victorious, but the king of Judah Jehoshaphat insisted on hearing from this one prophet called Micaiah.

> *15 Then he came to the king; and the king said to him, "Micaiah, shall we go to war against Ramoth Gilead, or shall we refrain?" And he answered him, "Go and prosper, for the Lord will deliver it into the hand of the king!"*
> *16 So the king said to him, "How many times shall I make you swear that you tell me nothing but the truth in the name of the Lord?"*
>
> 1 Kings 22:15-16

Micaiah was hesitant to say what God revealed to him because he knew it would bring about controversy so much that King Jehoshaphat had to compel him to tell his prophecy. Of course, Micaiah got persecuted and accused of being a false prophet, to the degree that one of the other prophets that got it wrong (Hezekiah, son of Chenaanah) slapped him for revealing that a lying spirit had inspired the rest of them to prophesy wrongly.

> *17 Then he said, "I saw all Israel scattered on the mountains, as sheep that have no shepherd. And the Lord said, 'These have no master. Let each return to his house in peace.'"*
>
> *18 And the king of Israel said to Jehoshaphat, "Did I not tell you he would not prophesy good concerning me, but evil?"*
>
> 1 Kings 22:17-18

Fake or False Prophets

You may ask, what about the case of false prophets? Didn't the bible say we should test the prophets and call out the false ones? You are right to have those questions because we are to grow in spiritual discernment to be able to identify the fakes. Every child of God can have access to one of the nine gifts of the spirit called the gift of discerning of spirits.

This gift will help you discern the spirit a person is operating under as they prophesy.

So, what are we to do about the fakes? I can answer that by sharing how bank staff are trained to identify and reject fake currency by simply not paying attention to the fake notes but rather study the original banknotes. They spend a lot of time studying original banknotes and develop the ability to detect original notes to the extent that they can easily point out a fake one. Likewise, the body of Christ is to spend quality time studying the office of the prophet and the operations of original, and authentic prophets to the point that it is easy to spot the false prophets.

We must be careful not to throw the baby out with the dirty bathwater. As long as the devil is still on earth influencing the heart of men, we would have false prophets. Do not accidentally disqualify and kill the authentic ones because you fear being fooled by the fakes and remember to acknowledge prophets that have been around for years and have been quite accurate with their past prophecies. Do not be quick to judge them because they have given one word that has not panned out the way we expected and at the time we thought they should manifest.

After the inauguration of the new US president in January 2021, some authentic prophets with good track records came

> As long as the devil is still on earth influencing the heart of men, we would have false prophets.

under attack by many Christians. I was so bothered one day that I jumped on my social media platform to record a short video to warn those within my space about the danger of killing our prophets. May God have mercy on us.

Don't Let Pharaohs Become Prophets

Another revelation I received from the Holy Spirit concerning the contention between the Pharaoh and Moses was that both were acting as prophets. Moses was God's appointed spokesman speaking God's word concerning the freedom of the Hebrews. On the other hand, Pharaoh who was a god to himself was prophesying that the Hebrews will not be released from slavery.

During their first clash of words, it looked like Pharaoh's words prevailed over Moses'. Moses said God had instructed him to prophesy to Pharaoh that he had to let His people go. Pharaoh on the other hand responded by prophesying that the Hebrews will have to endure more hardship instead.

Then the king of Egypt said to them, "Moses and Aaron, why do you take the people from their work? Get back to your labour." 5 And Pharaoh said, "Look, the people of the land are many now, and you make them rest from their labour!" 6 So the same day Pharaoh commanded the taskmasters of the people and their officers, saying, 7 "You shall no longer give the people straw to make brick as before. Let them go and gather straw for themselves. [8] And you shall lay on them the quota of bricks which they made before. You shall not reduce it. For they are idle; therefore, they cry out, saying, 'Let us go and sacrifice to our God.' [9] Let more work be laid on the men, that they may labour in it, and let them not regard false words."

Exodus 5:4-9

If you study Pharaoh's words carefully, you will notice that not only was he prophesying his preferred outcome, he also called Moses a false prophet. He referred to the prophetic word given by Moses as "false words". Now imagine the reaction of the elders when Pharaoh's harsh words came back to them. It was easy for the devil to convince them that Pharaoh was the true prophet as the taskmasters immediately began to enforce Pharaoh's words.

[13] And the taskmasters forced them to hurry, saying, "Fulfill your work, your daily quota, as when there was straw." [14] Also the officers of the children of Israel, whom Pharaoh's taskmasters had set over them, were beaten and were asked, "Why have you not fulfilled your task in making brick both yesterday and today, as before?"

Exodus 5:13-14

It was also easy for the Hebrews to consider Moses' words as false because Pharaoh did the opposite of letting them go. Nevertheless, they would have been wrong to call

100

Moses a false prophet, even worse, if they had killed Moses, they would have ended up with Pharaoh as the only prophet that will keep speaking over their lives. For this reason, it is extremely dangerous to attack and kill God's prophets.

In the absence of the ministry of the authentic prophets, the Pharaohs become the prophets speaking over the people. Remember that we learned earlier that Pharaohs can be a type of wealthy, powerful, and influential men that can make things happen just by speaking the word. Today I can see some 21st century Pharaohs acting like prophets. This revelation hit me after seeing a couple of articles written by mainstream media as well as videos on major digital platforms like YouTube.

> In the absence of the ministry of the authentic prophets...

The articles and videos had titles like, "The Top Ten Predictions of xxx that has come through" or "Five Major Predictions of xxx in 2021". Of course, 'xxx' represents the name of one of the powerful men I refer to as Pharaohs. Some of these men have been interviewed by major TV networks since the virus outbreak and economic calamities started. They have become the voice that many in the world listen to regarding the crisis today.

One particular 21st century Pharaoh who is neither a medical practitioner nor a pharmacologist has become a major voice on how to deal with the pandemic, vaccines and make claims about when he believes the world will come out of the global pandemic.

It is interesting to observe that some Christians have begun to order their lives in line with these prophecies from a non-Christian with no God-given prophetic gift. As I mentioned earlier, in the absence of authentic prophets, Pharaohs will become the prophets. That they have the wealth and power to influence certain outcomes after predicting it does not mean that they are to be received as prophets. My warning to you is that you be careful not to let Pharaohs become your prophet.

Believe God's Prophets and Prosper

Another lesson that the Holy Spirit has been teaching me in recent times is regarding understanding the benefits of believing God's prophets. As there are negative consequences when we do not believe God's prophets, there are also positive benefits when we believe them. To believe a prophet is to come into agreement with the message God has given him or her for you, unfortunately, many do not understand the power of agreement with a prophetic word.

They think that when a prophetic word is given, you leave it hanging in the air and watch to see if it happens or not. The people of Judah had to learn the lesson about the benefits of believing God's prophet at a time of national crisis. Whether they prospered at war or not was dependent on how they received the words of God's prophets.

²⁰ So they rose early in the morning and went out into the Wilderness of Tekoa; and as they went out, Jehoshaphat stood and said, "Hear me, O Judah and you inhabitants of Jerusalem: Believe in the LORD your God, and you shall be established; believe His prophets, and you shall prosper."

2 Chronicles 20:20

Jehoshaphat reinforced the truth that prosperity was a major benefit of believing God's prophet. The bible particularly the Old Testament is full of other stories of divine interventions through the ministry of a prophet that caused a person or people to experience prosperity. Stories like that of the widow of Zarephath in 1 Kings chapter seventeen and the Shunammite woman in 2 Kings allude to this. To stay in line with the main characters of this book, let me revisit the benefit that the children of Israel enjoyed for believing the words of the prophet God sent to them.

> To believe a prophet is to come into agreement with the message God has given him or her for you

The benefit of believing an unusual prophetic instruction as seen in Exodus chapter twelve led to their acquisition of great material wealth. Moses instructed the children of Israel to go borrow articles of value from the Egyptians as they prepared to go and those who believed the prophet did so and prospered. They came out of Egypt full.

Prayer:

Father, I thank you for the revelation of the superiority of the power of the kingdom of God over the devil and his cohorts.

I pray for the prophets in the body of Christ to be strong and effective in the battles they must fight.

I pray that men and women who have been seduced to become pharaohs will repent and surrender to the lordship of Jesus.

May your kingdom come, and your will be done on earth. May your grace be sufficient for me and your strength made perfect in my weakness to do my part on earth in Jesus' name. Amen!

CHAPTER 7

TAKE BACK WHAT THE PHARAOH STOLE

35 Now the children of Israel had done according to the word of Moses, and they had asked from the Egyptians articles of silver, articles of gold, and clothing. 36 And the LORD had given the people favour in the sight of the Egyptians, so that they granted them what they requested. Thus, they plundered the Egyptians.

Exodus 12:35-36

ONE THING I HAVE observed about God is that He hates injustice. Not only does he use His might to defend those who are oppressed and cheated among His children, He also believes in recompense as His word makes it clear that when He delivers, He also restores whatever had been stolen from His children.

³⁰ People do not despise a thief If he steals to satisfy himself when he is starving. ³¹ Yet when he is found, he must restore sevenfold; He may have to give up all the substance of his house.

Proverbs 6:30-31

According to God's standard, when a thief is caught, he should be made to pay back sevenfold what he stole meaning that damages paid must be more than what was stolen. The big challenge with many Christians is that we sometimes lack the revelation of what belongs to us.

Revelation of What Belongs to You

Recently I had to speak to some of my church leaders about a new inventory exercise. I wanted to have our church facility content insurance policy renewed and discovered that we needed to send an updated inventory list. Knowing that if we do not carry out this exercise, we may not be able to account for or prove what we own in the event of a fire outbreak or burglary, this updated inventory list was to give us as well as the insurance company knowledge of what our church owns.

Imagine if we had a burglary incident, one of the first questions the police would ask us is what was taken, without the list we might be able to spot the large or easily visible items but for sure we would not know all that was stolen. Besides, if the burglars were ever caught, we would still need to prove to the police that the items recovered belonged to us.

For God's children, our inventory lists are in the bible which is not just a historical or spiritual book. It also contains the testament of our heavenly Father and His Son Jesus. God through many of His spirit-inspired authors of the bible provided us with this information in several scriptural verses. Here are a few from the New Testament based on the finished work of Jesus on the cross.

> *9 For you know the grace of our Lord Jesus Christ, that though He was rich, yet for your sakes He became poor, that you through His poverty might become rich.*
>
> 2 Corinthians 8:9

> *8 And God is able to make all grace abound toward you, that you, always having all sufficiency in all things, may have an abundance for every good work.*
>
> 2 Corinthians 9:8

> *31 What then shall we say to these things? If God is for us, who can be against us? 32 He who did not spare His own Son, but delivered Him up for us all, how shall He not with Him also freely give us all things?*
>
> Romans 8:31-32

12 saying with a loud voice:
"Worthy is the Lamb who was slain to receive power
and riches and wisdom, And strength and honour and
glory and blessing!"

Revelation 5:12

The few verses above were chosen because they go beyond highlighting individual items that are usually on our need or want list. These verses reveal the vastness of the provision that the Father made for us and listed in His testament. In them, you will notice phrases like "all things", "all authority", "riches and the blessings". These words and phrases help to reveal that these promises of God are loaded.

Whenever you consider the gift of salvation that Jesus purchased for us with his blood, you should take note of the full meaning of the word 'salvation'. It comes from the Greek word 'Soteria' which means deliverance, preservation, safety and the sum of benefits and blessings which Christians, redeemed from all earthly ills, enjoy. In other words, all saved children of God have been given access to everything and anything that we need on earth to live life to the fullest till it overflows to bless others.

10 The thief comes only in order to steal and kill and destroy. I came that they may have and enjoy life, and have it in abundance (to the full, till it overflows).

John 10:10 AMP

108

We were brought out of darkness into light, from death to life and from poverty to unquantifiable wealth and riches. Therefore, I would like to state that whenever a child of God is lacking any of these things listed in the salvation package, it means that this child of God has been robbed. A thief had come and stolen what belonged to that child of God and he or she must be willing to fight to get it back.

In the recent season of the virus outbreak, so much has been stolen from people around the world. Unfortunately, many children of God's have made losses too with restricted freedom of movement, travel and of visiting people as we desire.

Some have lost family members who died prematurely while others lost their peace and joy as they have been bound by the spirit of fear unleashed around the world. Still, others have lost their income from employment or business enterprise and as a result, many have had their finances and material belongings devoured.

What has worried me the most is the level of ignorance among badly pastored believers who did not know what belonged to them by spiritual inheritance and hence did not put up a fight when the enemy started his stealing raid.

Some pastors who were supposed to teach their congregants to stand on God's word and contend for what was theirs exposed their fears in their online preaching and on their social media posts. Some closed their churches to their congregants for about a year because of the level of fear in them and made excuses that they were doing it to keep their congregants safe. The truth is that they did not know that divine protection, safety, healing and wholeness were theirs to keep. The thief was never supposed to be allowed to steal those from them.

Who Is in Possession of My Wealth?

One interesting discovery I got from the Holy Spirit is that the devil and his cohorts cannot take anything they have stolen away from the earth realm because of their illegal status in the earth.

> *"Most assuredly, I say to you, he who does not enter the sheepfold by the door, but climbs up some other way, the same is a thief and a robber.* [2] *But he who enters by the door is the shepherd of the sheep.*
>
> John 10:1-2

The legal access door into this earth is through being born of a woman. Therefore, the Son of God had to be conceived of the Holy Spirit and born through the womb of a woman. Every person on earth without a body is an illegal alien and has no legal rights on it. The best they can do is to try to reward their human agents with these stolen goods.

Let me use an analogy that you can easily understand. Imagine an illegal immigrant in the UK that begins to make money through criminal activities like drug trafficking. One challenge that this person will have is the ability to openly keep or spend this ill-gotten wealth. At best, this illegal criminal will try to launder the money and end up giving it to their partners (agents) that have legal status to help them keep or invest it.

The thief called Lucifer and his cohorts have mastered the art of giving the wealth that belongs to God's children to wicked sinners. They do that with the hope that these individuals will help carry out more evil deeds with this wealth rather than the good deeds that God's children will do with them.

I want you to understand that all that belongs to you as a child of God is still in this earth realm. You can get your money back; you can get your joy back; you can get your healing and wholeness back; you can get your protection and safety back. What you must do is identify the thief and then use your God-given weapons of warfare to take back what the enemy has stolen from you.

> ...Do not buy into the lie of a 'new normal' with losses of what you used to own.

Whatever you do, do not buy into the lie of a 'new normal' with losses of what you used to own. When the media started using the phrase 'new normal' in 2020, it was a way of stating that our lives will not get back to what they used to be before the virus outbreak. What many did not pay attention

111

to which the Holy Spirit revealed to me was that it was also the enemy's way to get people to settle for a future life with less than what they used to have.

So, I made up my mind and preached to my congregation to believe that we would have a new normal with the same privileges and belongings as before at the very least. I believed the crisis was our opportunity to grow in grace, strength, faith, anointing and manifestations of the blessing of God on our lives because when the Hebrews left Egypt after a season of devastating plagues, they did so with much more than what they used to possess before the plagues.

They came out with their health intact, animals intact, freedom from slavery and most importantly more wealth than they had ever possessed. I pray that this will be the portion of all born again children of God alive today.

Divine Assistance to Plunder Pharaoh and Egypt

When it comes to the subject of restoration, God's children come under a few different groups. The first group is made up of those who do not know that they lost anything and hence are oblivious to the need for restoration. The second group consist of those who know they have lost some of their belongings but do not know that they can have them back. The third group is made up of people who know they can recover what was stolen but do not know how to go about the recovery or restoration process.

The fix for God's children in group one and two is for them to get the revelation of what legally belongs to them and God's desire to see what was stolen restored as discussed earlier. For group three, the key is to understand that you need God's divine intervention to recover what was stolen because thieves do not enjoy giving back what they stole. You must make them and to do that you need superior powers to get them to cave in and give up what they stole.

In the case of the Israelites, they have been through at least a couple of centuries of slavery during which they had lost quite a lot of what God had given them through their ancestors Abraham, Isaac and Jacob. Here is a list of some of what they had lost by the time Moses was sent to them.

- Material wealth
- Financial independence
- Freedom to choose a vocation.
- Freedom of movement and travel
- Identity as Jehovah's covenant children
- Self-worth and self-dignity

You can now understand better what I meant when I said Pharaoh (being the thief that had robbed them) would not easily give back the things he had taken from them, they needed divine assistance from God.

Afterward Moses and Aaron went in and told Pharaoh,
"Thus says the LORD God of Israel: 'Let My people go,

113

that they may [a]hold a feast to Me in the wilderness.' "

Exodus 5:1-2

Moses was God's tool to bring the divine assistance they needed to get their belongings back. Once again, I want to state that the plagues were not meant to kill the covenant children of God but rather to display God's might and get Pharaoh to back off them and restore to them that he had stolen. Moses was able to boldly declare that they would not leave any belongings behind in Egypt because he knew that Jehovah was providing the divine assistance that he needed.

24 Then Pharaoh called to Moses and said, "Go, serve the LORD; only let your flocks and your herds be kept back. Let your little ones also go with you."
25 But Moses said, "You must also give [a]us sacrifices and burnt offerings, that we may sacrifice to the LORD our God. 26 Our livestock also shall go with us; not a hoof shall be left behind. For we must take some of them to serve the LORD our God, and even we do not know with what we must serve the LORD until we arrive there."

Exodus 10:24-26

Coming Out Full

The most beautiful aspect of the story of the Pharaoh, the Prophet and the Plagues is what happened at the end of the contentions and battles. Moses and the children of Israel did

114

not leave Egypt the same way as their descendants came in four hundred years before. They left Egypt full.

God fulfilled the promise He made to His prophet when He sent him out to battle with Pharaoh. Also, God has promised all His children alive today that when we are ready to leave this earth, we would leave full of life. Make up your mind to never settle for less than all the Father gave His Son to die on the cross to secure for you.

Prayer:
Father, I thank you for the revelation of my belongings through the work of Jesus your son. Thank you for paying the price for me to have it all.

Today I repent for limiting you in my mind and settling for less than what you had in mind for me. I henceforth arise in faith and promise to take back all that is mine. I will come out of every adversity, including pandemics and economic calamities full.

I pray that your grace will be sufficient for me and your strength will be made perfect in my weakness in Jesus' name. Amen!

MORE BOOKS BY
DANIEL OLUGBENGA MATEOLA

DANIEL OLUGBENGA MATEOLA

The Redemption Buffet

Possessing All Jesus Died To Recover For You

Foreword by Pastor Matthew Ashimolowo

DANIEL OLUGBENGA MATEOLA

FROM THE
RAT RACE
TO THE
GOD
RACE

How To Live The Life of Purpose & Fulfillment
That God Planned For You

UNDERSTANDING THE GOSPEL OF THE KINGDOM OF GOD

DANIEL MATEOLA

Daniel Matecla

daniel@kfmi.org.uk

+44 7984 420556

Whats App

Printed in Great Britain
by Amazon